A
Hole
in
the
Sidewalk

The Recovering Person's
Guide to Relapse Prevention

Claudia Black, Ph.D

ISBN No. 0-910223-27-0
A Hole in the Sidewalk
© 2000 by Claudia Black

Cover Design by Lin Kamer-Walker

Published by
MAC Publishing

PMB 346, 321 High School Rd. NE
Bainbridge Island, WA 98110 USA
206.842.6303
www.claudiablack.com

Dedication

I offer this page for a moment of reflection in honor of my friends and clients who have struggled to recover from their addictions. For many, the problem has been chemical dependency; for others, an addiction to spending, gambling, food, sex, love and relationships, or work. While the substance or behavior may differ, the process of the active disease is frequently similar. Regardless of addiction or disorder, relapse is common. I offer this work with respect for the insidiousness of the disease, the miracle of recovery, and the need for action.

A special thank you to—

Charlie Walker, Sandi Klein, and Jack Fahey. You have worked with me and supported me throughout this endeavor.

Autobiography
in Five ShortChapters

by Portia Nelson

I

I walk down the street.
There is a deep hole in the sidewalk.
I fall in.
I am lost . . . I am helpless.
It isn't my fault.
It takes forever to find a way out.

II

I walk down the same street.
There is a deep hole in the sidewalk.
I pretend I don't see it.
I fall in again.
I can't believe I am in the same place
but it isn't my fault.
It still takes a long time to get out.

III

I walk down the same street.
There is a deep hole in the sidewalk.
I see it is there.
I still fall in . . . it's a habit.
My eyes are open.
I know where I am.
It is my fault.
I get out immediately.

IV

I walk down the same street.
There is a deep hole in the sidewalk.
I walk around it.

V

I walk down another street.

Dear Readers,

In over twenty years of my work in the addictions field, I have had the honor of witnessing thousands of men and women of every age recover from various addictive disorders. Many are fortunate to remain abstinent from their first day of recovery, but there are those who relapse after several weeks, several months or even after years of abstinence. While I have met people who have relapsed at each phase, one of my most vivid memories was in working with a man who had been clean from alcohol for thirty years. Within just three days of starting to drink again, he needed to be hospitalized because he was so physically sick. Just as significant, he was as spiritually and emotionally bankrupt as he had been thirty years previously when he first quit drinking. Thus, the severe consequences of a relapse. Many people die in relapse, others remain chronic relapsers. Others who relapse eventually return to a program of recovery and find continuous sobriety.

While the most prevalent substance addictions are to alcohol and other drugs, this workbook can be utilized for a wide range of addictive disorders — from nicotine, alcohol and drug addictions, to sex, work, spending, gambling, food, and relationship addictions. The common theme in relapse is the resumption of self-destructive behaviors. Being an addict, in and of itself, means one is prone to relapse. To assume and simply hope it will not occur is denial. We must all take a proactive stance. Addictions are diseases of isolation and recovery begins with connecting to others who can help us understand our addiction, offer a path for recovery, and provide hope. Recovery is also about being accountable and taking action. Picking up this book is a statement that you take your addiction seriously and want to be proactive against a possible relapse. Whether or not you have a history of relapsing or want to immediately begin to work at potential stumbling blocks, this book can be a major asset.

It is my hope that if you have picked up "A Hole in the Sidewalk," you are already involved in a recovery process. The single greatest contributor to relapse is to lose sight of recovery as the first priority in life. Without recovery, all will be jeopardized — be it our relationship with God, our family, our job. Irrespective of importance, all are threatened if we cannot stay in recovery. If you are not involved in a recovery process, then please immediately seek a resource in your community that can give you direction as to what is available to you. **This book is not meant to be a program of recovery. It is meant to be an additional tool for your recovery.**

As previously acknowledged, people relapse at different phases in their recovery and for very different reasons. Knowing this, I have chosen to address various issues that I believe are often overlooked, or need to be reinforced. Most people will use this book as a workbook and start from the beginning. If you choose, after you have completed the first section ("Getting Started — A Look Over Your Shoulder") you can skip to the various themes that explore the issues you identify to be a priority. Please do not limit your responses to the numbers or lines offered. You may find it helpful to use a journal. I encourage you to share what you are learning about yourself with a counselor, therapist, sponsor or, recovering friend.

Depending on the addiction, the language that signifies recovery includes words such as clean and sober, abstinence, sobriety, etc. To be inclusive of the many possible addictions, I have chosen to use the word recovery. I ask you, the reader, to identify those behaviors that represent relapse, as well as recovery, from your own addiction(s).

Each section offers additional tools for your recovery. To remind you that knowledge about addiction and recovery is a tool, at the close of each section there is a toolbox icon. The more tools you gather and use, the more your recovery will be strengthened.

A very powerful tool is to acknowledge why we are grateful for our recovery everyday. Each section concludes with an opportunity to stop and reflect — not just on the exercises completed, but the day. In recovery, we often talk about the need to live *One Day at a Time*. Recovery, *One Day at a Time*, is a *gift* — that is why it is called the *present*. It is my hope that the moment for reflection will be something you include in your daily practice.

You will quickly see that I have a bias towards Twelve Step recovery. No other singular resource has been so instrumental in helping great numbers of people recover from various addictive disorders. If you choose not to utilize the Twelve Step programs you will still find this book helpful. I strongly encourage you to look at your resistances and be more open, and/or actively seek another avenue that will support you in recovery. I know of no other life threatening illness that is as treatable as addiction. At the back of the book you will find a listing of websites and telephone numbers for many programs and resources.

My hope for all addicted people is that they find recovery.

Know I am with you in spirit.

Claudia Black

Table of Contents

Getting Started—
A Look Over Your Shoulder

While we recognize the power addiction has had in our life, this concept needs to stay at the forefront of our consciousness. Addictive thinking can have us "off and running" before we are even ready for the start. "Getting Started" is an exercise that allows us to become centered and focused before we dive into the issues.

Answer the following questions as honestly as possible. Remember, there are no right or wrong answers, only your answers.

When did you first start engaging in your addictive behavior(s)?

> When we moved to our new house in Va. Beach in Sept of 1962, I was 10 years old. I started running with the Lewis boys + my brother. We built forts with stolen construction materials + started stealing beers + cigarettes by the time I was 11½. By the time I was 13, I loved to run, steal, smoke, drink beer, play strip poker in the woods.

Describe the history and progression of your addictive behavior up to the present date.

> By the time I was 16, I was going to bars. I was very active, so I didn't drink all the time or get drunk + pass out often, but by the time I was 20, I did. Around then, I discovered pot, acid and painkillers, but I preferred beer. Around the time my Mom died when I was 25, my husband, Steve + I drank daily, fought and used codeine, valium, quaaludes, cocaine + crank steadily. When I turned 30, I just could not continue to play music and drink every night and tried to commit suicide. I broke up our band, started counselling + antidepressants

Review the previous response and note negative consequences to your behavior.

_____

_____

_____

_____

The following examples reflect both powerlessness and unmanageability. If you have difficulty naming consequences, these examples will be helpful.

Obsessed or fantasized about addictive behavior	Involved in other destructive behavior against self or others
Tried to control behavior	Felt guilty or shameful about behaviors
Lied, covered up, or minimized behavior	Experienced depression
Tried to rationalize behavior	Broke promises to self or others
Physical health affected	Negative feelings about self
Emotional health affected	Denied I have a problem
Social life affected	Gave up my hobbies and interests
Parenting skills affected	Primary relationship affected
Involved in accidents or other dangerous situations	Work or school life affected
Had contact with police or courts	Financial situation affected
Spirituality affected	Manipulated people into supporting my addictions

Powerlessness and Unmanageability

Powerlessness implies being unable to stop the behavior despite obvious consequences. List examples that show how powerless you are to stop your behaviors. Be very explicit about types of behaviors and frequencies. Start with your earlier examples and conclude with your most recent.

Examples: Continued to use despite girlfriend leaving

Continued to drive despite having a suspended license for DUI

Continued to see boyfriend in spite of abuse

Continued to purge in spite of related dental problems

1) _____

2) _____

3) _____

4) _____

5) _____

6) _____

7) _____

8) _____

9) _____

10) _____

11) _____

12) _____

13) _____

14) _____

15) _____

To reinforce powerlessness and unmanageability, list as many examples as you can think of that show how your life has become totally unmanageable because of your dependency.

Unmanageability means that your addiction created chaos and damage in your life.

Examples: Six months ago I was caught stealing to support my habit

I had to declare bankruptcy because I maxed out my credit cards buying drugs

My wife left me because I had multiple affairs

I lost my job for calling in sick too many times

I put God out of my life

My husband took the kids because too many times I put them in dangerous situations

1) _____

2) _____

3) _____

4) _____

5) _____

6) _____

7) _____

8) _____

9) _____

10) _____

11) _____

12) _____

13) _____

14) _____

15) _____

Do you have a desire to stop engaging in your addictive behavior?

☐ Yes   ☐ No

If yes, list the specific benefits to recovery.

1) _____

2) _____

3) _____

4) _____

5) _____

6) _____

7) _____

8) _____

What difficulties do you anticipate with recovery?

1) _____

2) _____

3) _____

4) _____

5) _____

How would life look in recovery?

_____

_____

_____

Recognize powerlessness
Recognize unmanageability of addiction
Aware of being an addict
Identify hope

Today, I am grateful for _____

Hey ... No Problem

Overconfidence is a major threat to recovery. Addicts believe they have the abilities to handle situations without respect for the dangers of addiction. But seemingly harmless actions result in grave consequences. Signs of overconfidence include:

- Calling your own shots
- Inability to hear what others are saying
- Feeling contempt prior to investigation
- Wanting immediate results and having unrealistic expectations

Calling your own shots is the first sign of overconfidence. When we first entered into recovery, we may have attended numerous meetings, established a relationship with a sponsor, and started to build a support system.

As time in recovery progresses, we probably begin to feel better about ourselves and our life in recovery. Once we feel better, it becomes easy to reject what others are suggesting. We often begin to replay those old tapes. "I know what is really best for me" or "I can do it by myself, I have for all these years and I am still alive." Such people in Twelve Step recovery meetings are called "yes, butters"— "Yes, but I am not like those people, yet." "Yes, but I am not dead, yet." "Yes, but I have not lost my wife, yet." "Yes, but I have not lost my job, yet."

In essence, we are ready to take back total control of our life. This demonstrates the power of the addictive process and the grandiose thinking that we as addicts regularly engage in. To paraphrase an Alcoholics Anonymous saying, "My best thinking kept me drinking, drugging, gambling, etc." We forget what we learned in the First Step of any Twelve Step recovery program: "We admitted we were powerless over our addictive behaviors and that our lives had become unmanageable."

Inability to hear what others are saying is the second sign of overconfidence. **Has this happened to you?** You were in a self-help group meeting and discounted what others were saying because you knew yourself best. We are so well practiced at listening to our own voice of denial and justification that we are unable to absorb input from outside sources. Again, we often think, "My situation is different." "I was sober for about two years," Francine shared. "Then, my old friends invited me to a birthday party. I called my sponsor who told me to avoid the party. I went anyway because I had confidence in myself. When I got there, everybody was using. Before long, I found myself thinking…maybe this time…. That was when I relapsed."

Feeling contempt prior to investigation is the third sign of overconfidence. Here, we discount methods of recovery that have often proven effective. **Has this happened to you?** It is suggested that we go to a Narcotics Anonymous or another Twelve Step meeting. After the first fifteen minutes of the meeting, we decide this meeting is not for us. No one there had anything to offer us. Or, we didn't even bother to try the meeting out. We rejected the idea without any investigation. "I wasn't like those people around me. I hadn't lost everything to my addictions, ended up divorced, lost my house, or anything like that. I left Twelve Step meetings because I couldn't identify with how sick those people really were."

Wanting immediate results and having unrealistic expectations is the fourth and final sign of overconfidence. We, as addicts, want results right now. This is especially true for the addict whose pattern has been one of instant gratification. You may have said to yourself, "After all, I have been sober six months and my employer still hasn't given me back all of the responsibility that I once had." "My wife does not fully trust me around other women even though I was only unfaithful when I was using." (An aside, "I only used for the last 14 years.") "I haven't been below my required calorie limit for three weeks now; the doctor isn't being fair about saying it's dangerous to participate in my sport."

Our thinking here is, "I expect that because I have stayed sober, the world will give me what I want and will give it to me right now. If it doesn't, then why should I put all of this effort into my abstinence?" There is an attitude that the rest of the world owes us. In fact we may think, "I've got something coming. I should be rewarded because I have given up so much — my alcohol, drugs, sex, gambling, or other addictions."

This thinking is often known as "terminal uniqueness." We believe that our situation is different from everyone else's and that we deserve preferential treatment.

For most people, life in recovery does get better, but it takes time and it is not always in "our" time frame. Remember, recovery is a process — *not an event.* Recovery is the ability to genuinely recognize that others do have something of value to offer. None of us has all of the answers.

Point: "My best thinking got me here."

Rating Signs of Overconfidence

On a scale of one to ten, one meaning you least identify, ten meaning you most identify, rate yourself in the areas discussed.

Calling your own shots

1_____10

Inability to hear what others are saying

1_____10

Feeling contempt prior to investigation

1_____10

Wanting immediate results and having unrealistic expectations

1_____10

What did you learn?

_____

_____

_____

_____

_____

Are you talking about this in your home group? With a sponsor? With a counselor? The first step is recognizing how signs of overconfidence are problematic, the second step is holding the signs up for the light to shine through. Talk about it.

The following exercises will allow you to explore signs of overconfidence more thoroughly.

Calling Your Own Shots

Examples

My wife suggests I not attend a bachelor party; I go anyway.	Everybody was using; I found myself craving the drug.
I took an unnecessary additional project at work when I was already stressed; my sponsor had discouraged it.	I found myself making excuses to not attend recovery meetings.

Identify examples of calling your own shots	Identify the negative consequences
1)	1)
2)	2)
3)	3)
4)	4)
5)	5)

Inability to Hear What Others Are Saying

Examples

I was told not to drink alcohol, but being a cocaine addict, I thought that was ridiculous	Started drinking beer every night; after two weeks I was using cocaine.
It was suggested I not go into convenience stores as they could trigger my smoking and gambling.	Within four weeks I was rationalizing I could play the Lotto safely. Within eight weeks I was smoking again and gambling out of control.

Identify examples of inability to hear what others are saying	Identify the negative consequences
1)	1)
2)	2)
3)	3)
4)	4)
5)	5)

Feeling Contempt Prior to Investigation

Examples

I decided the female counselor I was supposed to see wouldn't understand me. Didn't even show up for the session. Don't know if she would have helped me or not.	Got back into negative thinking and sought out previous friends to support it.
I refuse to try meditation because I am not religious.	I don't find the serenity others seem to find.

Identify examples of contempt prior to investigation	Identify the negative consequences
1)	1)
2)	2)
3)	3)
4)	4)
5)	5)

Wanting Immediate Results

Examples

I expected my children to be all loving and supportive because I went to treatment.	I got angry with them when I didn't get the loving attitude I thought I should and used that as an excuse to justify my relapse.
I wanted a job at same salary level as others at my level of experience.	I refused lower paying jobs, didn't get work, couldn't pay any bills, got resentful, started acting out.

Identify examples of wanting immediate results with unrealistic expectations	Identify the negative consequences
1)	1)
2)	2)
3)	3)
4)	4)
5)	5)

Are you willing to address these issues openly?

☐ Yes   ☐ No

With whom and when will you discuss this?

_____

_____

_____

_____

_____

**Be patient
Have an open attitude
Can listen and hear
Have realistic expectations**

Today, I am grateful for _____

I've Got It

The addict went to the horse race and bet everything he had on this particular horse. The bell rings. As the race begins, he looks up into the sky and prays, "God, I really need you today. Please let me win this race and I promise I will never, ever, use drugs again." The horse is rounding the first curve and it is second to last. As the race goes into the backstretch, his is still not making any headway. The addict again says, "God, where are you? I really need you. Please let me win and I promise I will go to a meeting every night." As his horse hits the pole, it is still trailing behind all the others. "God, God, I will do service work the rest of my life." Suddenly the horse begins to move up in its standing. Within the last 100 feet, it is leading — a miracle. The alcoholic looks up to the sky and says, "That's okay God, I've got it now!"

Did you find this joke funny? Sad? True?

In essence, we say to ourselves, "I can't drink, use drugs safely, or engage in my other addictive behaviors — and I accept that. But what I don't accept is that I don't have control over other people, places, and things. The people, places, and things that I still try to control are my co-workers, my spouse, my kids, or the traffic light." The frustration and anger involved in trying to control so many things may quickly lead us back to our original, or to new addictive behaviors. Our controlling behavior leads us to believe that we can control our addiction(s). "I know I can't use cocaine anymore, but maybe I can start drinking. Drinking was never that bad for me." Or, "I can't gamble at the horse races but I could play the lottery." Or, "I know it's not wise for me to go to massage parlors, but pictures on the Internet won't hurt." These examples show how control leads to relapse.

Answer these two questions:

In what areas of your life are you having difficulty because you are trying to control that which you do not have the power to control?

_____

_____

_____

How would those close to you answer that question?

_____

_____

_____

_____

_____

Giving Up Control

Letting go of control in recovery is often extremely difficult to do. In order to embrace recovery, we need to surrender to the fact that we are powerless over people, places, and situations. In doing so, a great deal of fear may surface at what might happen if control were given up.

This exercise is designed to help identify what "letting go of control" would mean in your life.

Complete the following sentence stems.

Giving up control in my life would mean

1) _____

2) _____

3) _____

4) _____

5) _____

When I think about giving up control, I fear

1) _____

2) _____

3) _____

4) _____

5) _____

Control is often perceived as an all-or-nothing issue. Many of us have fears resulting from ideas about what it means to give up control. Some examples of these perceptions are:

> I will be angry, become violent, hostile or mean
> I feel that I may physically hurt someone
> I will lose friendships and offend others
> My partner will leave
> I won't be heard
> I won't be a real man/woman
> I will start to cry and not be able to stop
> I will let go of my rage and break furniture or hurt people

Look at the statements you wrote regarding losing control. Where do those thoughts and feelings come from? How old are they? How likely is it that those fears will be realized? So often our fears are greater than the reality.

List the negative consequences of your controlling behavior.

1) _____

2) _____

3) _____

4) _____

5) _____

Learning to let go of control takes time. It is not an all-or-nothing proposition. As addicts, we often think in black or white with nothing in between. In recovery, when we talk about letting go of control, we mean letting go of *some* control. Learning to not think in terms of all-or-nothing takes time. The Serenity Prayer of Alcoholics Anonymous discusses "Courage to change the things I can." This means that not everything can or even needs to be changed at once. Recovery takes time. It is a lifelong process, *"One Day at a Time."*

Below is the Serenity Prayer. It helps to remind us that we don't have control over every event or person in our lives. It also reminds us that we can change *some* situations in our lives. By saying the Serenity Prayer, we are asking for wisdom and guidance from our Higher Power to helping us distinguish between these two.

The Serenity Prayer

God,
Grant me the serenity to accept the things I cannot change
Courage to change the things I can
And the wisdom to know the difference

It is not suggested that we are being asked to give up all control, but to give consideration to the word *some*. As we let go of some control, we actually become more empowered. We will find flexibility where there has only been rigidity. When we begin to let go of some control, we begin to experience that which we have been searching for. We find as we let go of control, we have the opportunity to relax, to play, and to not carry the burden of the world on our shoulders. We have the opportunity to know ourselves better, to be honest with others and ourselves — to trust, to listen, and to connect. It is when we let go of control that this process also takes on spiritual meaning. We cannot experience a spiritual healing process until we are willing to let go of control.

List the positive consequences to letting go of some control.

1) _____

2) _____

3) _____

4) _____

5) _____

Have faith
Live in the process

Today, I am grateful for _____

I'll Handle This

Letting go of self-will means letting go of control. It is the manipulation of people, places, and objects. Controlling behavior is about many things.

- Controlling behavior can be a response to shame. It compensates for our inner belief that says, "I am not adequate, I am insufficient, I am damaged." We may have carried this message with us for most of our lives.

- Controlling behavior gives us a sense of power to compensate for the sense of powerlessness. It may be a false sense of power, but false or not, it is better than no power.

- Growing up in what was often a dysfunctional home, we may have learned from early on that the illusion of having *some* control in our chaotic environment was critical for survival. Control brings predictability.

However we learned it, we don't need to be critical of our control. We just need to recognize if it is interfering in our recovery today.

There are many styles of control. The four styles listed below are among the most common.

Sweet Controller — Sweet, polite, and pleasant. "And, I *always* get what I want."

Distant Controller — Emotionally cold, rigidly efficient, and a master of details.

Passive Controller — "I don't care. It doesn't matter to me. That is okay, but I will get you in the end." Otherwise known as the Martyr.

Angry Controller — "I want what I want when I want it. And I will darn well get it." The Intimidator.

What style(s) of control did your parents use?

_____

_____

What style(s) of control do you use today?

_____

_____

_____

Irrespective of the controlling style, controllers operate from a position of fear, shame, and distrust. We pay the consequences for our controlling behavior. We may not know how to listen or follow direction. We may lack in creativity or spontaneity. We may withhold thoughts and feelings, and we often intimidate people. Control is a major barrier to recovery. Faith and control don't peacefully coexist. If you are searching for intimacy, you can't have it without letting go of control.

Trying to be in control has left us very angry or depressed because our needs cannot be met. Despite our best efforts to control, we often find ourselves frustrated and resentful because our efforts to control have failed — *again*.

In order to let go of attempting to control events and other people in our lives, we need to increase our understanding of our responsibility for our feelings and actions.

Letting Go of Self Will

As you answer these questions, rate yourself on a scale of one to ten, one meaning the least and ten the most.

Are you unselfish or do you put your needs before the needs of others? If the latter, give an example.

Unselfish-1_____10-Selfish

_____

If you rated yourself 7 or above or 3 or less, do you think this area contributes to the possibility of relapse?

☐ Yes ☐ No

If yes, explain:

_____

_____

_____

Do you admit and take responsibility when you are wrong, or do you make excuses, justify, or blame others? If the latter, give an example.

       Responsible-1 _____10-Blame, justify

_____

Do you let go and forgive, or do you hold onto resentments and self-pity? If the latter, give an example.

       Forgiveness-1 _____10-Resentment

_____

_____

_____

Do you tend to deal with problems directly, or do you procrastinate or avoid dealing with problems? If the latter, give an example.

       Act-1 _____10-Avoid

_____

_____

_____

If you rated yourself 7 or above on any of these scales, do you think this area contributes to the possibility of relapse?

    ☐ Yes   ☐ No

Control

If yes, explain:

_____

_____

_____

If letting go of control is a problematic area, identify on a daily basis two areas you want to practice "letting go." It may be the same two areas repeatedly, but staying aware of your intent will help you to be able to follow through. One way to do this is to use the sentence stem, *Today I will let go of control of* _____ in a morning meditation.

Remember that each day in recovery, learning to let go of our need to control helps us to stay in the moment; to trust in our Higher Power; to accept that we don't have to have all the answers, have a plan for everything, or to control everything.

Can identify self will behaviors
Am accountable
Consider others
Am willing to let go
Identify controlling behaviors

Today, I am grateful for _____

Name That Feeling

Relapse Connection

Check the connections between your feelings and your addiction(s) that are most applicable:

- ☐ I engage in my addictive behavior(s) because I want my feelings to go away
- ☐ I engage in my addictive behavior(s) because I want to let my feelings out

Are there specific feelings you are trying to medicate or express? Name them.

_____

_____

Nick Nolte spoke the following words in the movie *Prince of Tides*.

> "I don't know when my parents began their war against each other, but I do know the only prisoners they took were their children. When (we) needed to escape, we developed a ritual— we found a silent soothing world where there was no pain, a world without mothers and fathers. But that was a long time ago, before I chose not to have a memory."

That silent, soothing world is what addictive disorders represent to many of us.

Alan, a 32-year-old addict, says, "I was eleven when I took my first drink. I hated the taste, but I felt the glow and it worked. I would get sick as a dog, but would still do it again. I got drunk because I had a hole in my gut so big and alcohol filled it up. Alcohol and drugs would become the solution. There was one reason I drank and used. It was to get blithering numb. And when I was numb, not a thing or person could hurt me; I felt nothing."

Often, the attraction to addictive behaviors was that they served to medicate our inner pain. For so many in recovery, abstaining from our addiction(s) results in experiencing something we have strived much of our life to stay away from — our feelings. In early recovery, it is the *fear of feeling* that will send many of us back to our addictive behaviors.

The ability to express and feel safe with feelings is something that is most often impeded at an early age. Many addicts grew up in dysfunctional or abusive homes where it was not safe to express feelings. As a result, we live with much fear, disappointment, sadness, and embarrassment. We witnessed anger, pain, and rage. It was a very lonely time. If we showed any feelings at all, we often were rejected. We were given such shaming messages as, "Big boys or girls don't cry," "Don't be such a sissy," or "I'll really give you something to cry about." A show of feelings was frequently met with disapproval, rejection, or even punishment. The message, whether delivered overtly or covertly, was very clear — "It is not okay to be your own person with individual feelings, desires, or needs." Feelings need to be avoided at all costs.

Recovery is the ability to tolerate feelings without needing to medicate them.

The following questions begin the process of understanding your "feeling" self.

What two feelings are the easiest to express in front of other people?

1) _____

2) _____

What are the two most difficult feelings to express in front of other people?

1) _____

2) _____

We often mask painful feelings with other emotions. For example, we may mask sadness with humor, fear with intellectualizing, anger with social isolation. By identifying when we use these defenses, we are a step closer to recognizing the underlying feeling.

Examine one of the difficult feelings you just identified. When you begin to experience this feeling, what do you do to mask or defend against it?

_____

_____

_____

_____

_____

Take a feeling you just described that you mask — one that is difficult for you to show others. Identify the fear(s) that gets in the way of your showing that feeling. Common fears are: "Someone will think I'm stupid." "People will take advantage of me." " I wouldn't be in control." What are your fears?

_____

_____

_____

Do not edit your thoughts. The fear comes from your personal history. For you, the fear is real. It is only by acknowledging the fear that we can put it to rest. More often than not, the fear is based in history rather than present-day realities. If you are frightened of sharing feelings, you need to ask yourself if you are carrying past experiences into the present. Sometimes we, as addicts, have a tremendous amount of unwarranted energy surrounding a situation. Should your fears be based in present-day experiences, then discuss with a safe person what needs to occur for those fears to be lessened.

Feelings

We have many feelings, some we are willing to expose to others, others we choose to keep hidden. Identify the feelings you experienced (whether or not you expressed them) in the age ranges indicated. The list of feelings is only a partial one; feel free to add your own.

People often have more than one feeling at a time, and those feelings may seem contrary to each other. One can love and hate, be sad and angry, be fearful and happy at the same time. This does not mean you are crazy; it means you have reasons to be fearful and happy, angry and sad, or to hate and love at the same time.

love	anger	bravery	confusion	anxiousness
hurt	gloom	shyness	happiness	embarrassment
fear	guilt	patience	moodiness	disappointment
hate	caring	jealousy	excitement	encouragement
worry	warmth	joy	frustration	discouragement
shame	sadness	resentment	loneliness	

Age	Expressed Feelings	Unexpressed Feelings
Before 12	_____	_____
	_____	_____
	_____	_____
12 to 17	_____	_____
	_____	_____
	_____	_____
18 to 24	_____	_____
	_____	_____
	_____	_____
25 to 34	_____	_____
	_____	_____
	_____	_____
35 to 44	_____	_____
	_____	_____
	_____	_____
45 to 54	_____	_____
	_____	_____
	_____	_____
55 to 64	_____	_____
	_____	_____
	_____	_____
65 +	_____	_____
	_____	_____
	_____	_____

What did you learn? _____

_____

_____

Identify feelings
Let go of defenses

Today, I am grateful for _____

The "F" Word: Fear

Many of us grew up with chronic fear. While frequently experienced, fear is often denied. These fears, recognized or not, are carried into adulthood. Our drug of choice is a great medicator. But once clean and sober, we become aware of the fear. This fear is referred to as "unidentifiable" or "free-floating" fear. In some instances, this fear becomes pervasive (ever-present) or may appear episodically (appearing quickly and powerfully, then disappearing almost as mysteriously).

Make a list of four situations that occurred while you were growing up that you remember as being fearful and note whether or not you expressed that fear.

1) _____

2) _____

3) _____

4) _____

Check the behaviors that describe what you did as a child when you felt afraid:

☐ Acted like I was not afraid

☐ Cried

☐ Got angry

☐ Hid (Where?) _____

☐ Told someone about my fear

☐ Other (fill in) _____

When I was afraid, my mom usually

☐ Never noticed

☐ Noticed, but ignored it

☐ Made me feel embarrassed or ashamed

☐ Made me feel better

☐ Other (fill in) _____

When I was afraid, my dad usually

- ☐ Never noticed
- ☐ Noticed, but ignored it
- ☐ Made me feel embarrassed or ashamed
- ☐ Made me feel better
- ☐ Other (fill in) _____

If there was a particular person — a brother, sister, or other significant person in your life — that responded to your fear (either negatively or positively), describe how they responded.

_____

_____

_____

Expressing Fear

To better understand how you experience fear as an adult, complete the following sentences:

When I am afraid, I

_____

_____

_____

_____

When I am afraid, I

_____

_____

_____

_____

If people knew I was afraid,

_____

_____

_____

_____

If people knew I was afraid,

_____

_____

_____

Fear Today

There are many valid reasons to feel fear, but these can be distorted by addictive thinking. You might find the following acronyms relevant to you: **FEAR**—**F**alse **E**vidence **A**ppearing **R**eal or **F**orget **E**verything **A**nd **R**un. If you identify with either of these, it will be helpful to use them as reminders of how addictive thinking can magnify feelings of fear or create needless fears.

In early recovery, the fears are many and include:

> If people really knew me they would reject me
> I'll never be good enough
> I'm too set in my ways to change
> My life is over

Complete the following exercise. Identify present day fears. On the right-hand side of the page, list people with whom you have shared the specific fear or you are willing to share that fear with now.

Today I feel afraid about:

Name

1) _____   _____

_____   _____

_____   _____

2) _____   _____

_____   _____

_____   _____

3) _____   _____

_____   _____

_____   _____

What are the positives of owning fear?

☐ Relief
☐ Being less controlled
☐ Greater physical health
☐ Not hiding pain
☐ Being more honest
☐ Other

**Identify and own fears
Know self better**

Today, I am grateful for _____

How Do You Plead—Guilty?

Guilt is a feeling of regret or remorse about something we have or have not done. While guilt is a healthy emotion that facilitates social conscience it is particularly distorted if we were raised in a dysfunctional family. Often when problems occur, family members blame each other — wives blame husbands, husbands blame wives, parents blame children, children blame parents, children blame each other. Young children, because they are defenseless, most readily accept and internalize the blame.

We may not be aware that we internalized guilt as intensely as we have until we see ourselves acting out the guilt by forever apologizing, chronically taking care of others at our expense, or having feelings of depression.

Childhood Guilt

Check the boxes of the family members about whom you felt guilt for things that took place when you were a child.

☐ Mom

_____

_____

☐ Dad

_____

_____

☐ Sister (name)

_____

_____

☐ Sister (name)

_____

_____

☐ Brother (name)

_____

_____

☐ Brother (name)

_____

_____

☐ Other (name)

_____

_____

☐ Other (name)

_____

_____

For each box checked, give two reasons that prompted your guilt. Example: "I felt responsible for Mom and Dad's arguing because they often argued about me." "I felt responsible for my brother getting hit—I was older—I should have been able to stop my dad." "I felt responsible for not being able to make my mom happier; I could have gotten better grades at school."

Check the behavior that describes what you did as a child when you felt guilty:

☐ Ate to stuff my feelings of guilt

☐ Hid (Where?) _____

☐ Apologized

☐ Cleaned the house

☐ Tried to act "real good"

☐ Other (fill in) _____

☐ Other (fill in) _____

When I felt guilty, my mom usually:

☐ Never knew

☐ Reinforced my guilt by blaming me for things I did not do

☐ Made me feel even guiltier

☐ Punished me even if I was not at fault

☐ Made me feel that I was not responsible, therefore, helping to lessen my guilt

☐ Other (fill in) _____

When I felt guilty, my dad usually:

☐ Never knew

☐ Reinforced my guilt by blaming me for things I did not do

☐ Made me feel even guiltier

☐ Punished me even if I was not at fault

☐ Made me feel that I was not responsible, therefore, helping to lessen my guilt

☐ Other (fill in) _____

What do you do when you feel guilty today?

_____

_____

_____

False Guilt

Because children have limited mental, physical, and emotional resources, a major part of parenting involves physically and psychologically protecting the children — allowing them to be "safe." As children, we need security, love, happiness and honesty in order to grow and feel good about ourselves. Yet in many homes, parents are not able to provide these needs on a consistent basis. In such families the child attempts to fill the void and assume parental responsibilities. But remember, these are young children — children who do not yet have the ability to act as responsible adults. Not only do parents often ask children to take responsibility for things that adults should normally be responsible for, they often insinuate that their children are the cause of their (the adults') problems. Children usually believe their parents know everything and accept their parents' every word. As a result, young children have a distorted view of their power. They come to believe they have power to affect people, places, and situations far more than they truly can. This results in a false sense of guilt and an overwhelming sense of powerlessness.

Do you come from a history of taking on false guilt?

☐ Yes ☐ No

Do you take on false guilt today?

☐ Yes ☐ No

If you answered yes, complete the following exercise.

Saying No To False Guilt

We often have a distorted perception of where our power lies and as a result live with much false guilt. True guilt is remorse or regret we feel for something we have or have not done. False guilt is taking on the feeling for someone else's behavior and actions. It is important to gain a realistic perspective of situations that we have the power to affect.

Because this is usually a lifelong habit, it is important to go back and delineate historically

Feelings

what we were and were not responsible for. That assists us in being more skilled in recognizing our lifelong pattern of assuming false guilt, and stopping it.

Reflect back on your childhood and adolescence, consider the things you feel guilty about and say no to each situation. Say, "No! I wasn't responsible for _____," "No! It wasn't my fault, my obligation."

Write "No!" in each blank and then continue by finishing the sentence:

_____, I was not responsible for _____

when he/she _____

_____, I was not responsible for _____

when he/she _____

_____, it wasn't my fault when _____

_____, it wasn't my fault when _____

_____, it wasn't my duty or obligation to _____

_____, it wasn't my duty or obligation to _____

_____, I was only partially responsible for _____

_____, I was only partially responsible for _____

What do you feel false guilt about today?
1) _____
2) _____
3) _____
4) _____
5) _____

Guilt Today

List the people and situations about which you feel guilt today.

Today I feel guilt about:

1) _____

_____

_____

2) _____

_____

_____

3) _____

_____

_____

While it is common to be confused about false guilt, the reality is that as addicts (irrespective of our addictions) we are responsible for our own behavior. In our addiction we have hurt other people.

- Cindy, a co-dependent, is guilty in not attending to her children's needs appropriately because she is following her addiction to relationships. She is preoccupied with where and when the next relationship will be occurring.

- Bill, an alcoholic, is guilty for continually lying to his partner and friends.

- Jake, a compulsive overeater, is guilty for his stealing.

- Jessica is guilty for her lying related to her gambling.

Step Eight in a Twelve Step Program says, "Made a list of all persons we had harmed, and became willing to make amends to them all." Step Nine says, "Made direct amends to such people whenever possible, except when to do so would injure them or others."

Have you completed Steps Eight and Nine in a Twelve Step program?

☐ Yes   ☐ No

If yes, how was your experience working these Steps?

_____

_____

_____

If you have completed these Steps, is it possible you omitted certain people?

☐ Yes ☐ No

If you haven't done these Steps, what has gotten in the way of doing them?

_____

_____

_____

Do you have a home group?

☐ Yes ☐ No

Do you have a sponsor?

☐ Yes ☐ No

There is an appropriate time and a place for making amends. Amends are not just verbal apologies. They are also expressed in the form of healthy behavior. For example, if you are feeling guilty about not previously showing up at your daughter's ballgame, you can show up at her ballgame today. If you are guilty for stealing from a relative's home, you can begin to make payments. If you are guilty for raging at family members, you can enroll in an anger management course.

Identify three behaviors that would facilitate you in making amends right now.

1) _____

2) _____

3) _____

What are the positives of owning guilt?

- ☐ Relief
- ☐ Being less controlled
- ☐ Greater physical health
- ☐ Not hiding pain
- ☐ Being more honest
- ☐ Other

Identify and own guilt
Know self better
Distinguish true from false guilt

Today, I am grateful for _____

Cry Me a River—or Drought

With loss there is sadness, and with sadness there are tears. Feeling sad and crying are a natural part of being human. If we did not receive validation for our sadness — if negative responses were experienced when expressing sadness — we probably began to control the expression of sadness. More likely than not, the way we express our sadness and all other feelings has been scripted since childhood. We find ourselves without the ability to cry. Or, we find that after years of seldom crying, we are frequently crying and are unable to identify the reasons for the over-abundance of tears.

The next few exercises are designed to enable you to identify your sadness and to help you to better understand how you perceive crying.

Past Sadness

In some families, certain things that were said or occurred caused sadness. In others sadness was caused by what wasn't said or what didn't occur. Our sadness may be caused by all of the times we had to move, a parent failing to attend school events, or from never being told that we were loved.

Complete the following sentence.

When I was a child or teenager, I can remember feeling sad about … (whether or not anyone else knew that you were sad):

1) _____

2) _____

3) _____

Check the behaviors that describe what you did as a child when you felt sad:

☐ Cried when I was alone

☐ Cried in front of others

- ☐ Went to bed
- ☐ Took a walk
- ☐ Told someone about my sadness
- ☐ Other (fill in) _____
- ☐ Other (fill in) _____

When I felt sad, my mom usually

- ☐ Never noticed
- ☐ Noticed, but ignored it
- ☐ Made me feel embarrassed or ashamed
- ☐ Made me feel better
- ☐ Other (fill in) _____

When I felt sad, my dad usually

- ☐ Never noticed
- ☐ Noticed, but ignored it
- ☐ Made me feel embarrassed or ashamed
- ☐ Made me feel better
- ☐ Other (fill in) _____

If there was a particular person — a brother, sister or other significant person in your life — that responded to your sadness (either negatively or positively), describe how they responded.

_____

_____

_____

Expressing Sadness Without Tears

This exercise is designed for us if we have difficulty expressing sadness with tears and if we fear our tears.

Complete the following sentences.

When I cry, I

_____

_____

_____

When I cry, I feel

_____

_____

_____

If people see me cry I

_____

_____

_____

If you were unable to complete the previous exercise because you never cry, complete the following statements.

I never cry because

_____

_____

_____

If I ever did cry, I would

_____

_____

_____

I might have felt better if I'd cried when

_____

_____

_____

Sadness Today

Addiction creates loss. Where there is loss there is sadness. We are often sad for our distant relationships with our children, for the pain the addiction has caused in our most intimate relationships, for how we have hurt our friends, or because a major part of our life is irretrievable.

Complete the following exercise. Identify present day sadness. On the right-hand side of the page, list people with whom you have shared the specific sadness with or you are willing to share that sadness with now.

Today I feel sad about: Name

1) _____   _____

   _____   _____

   _____   _____

2) _____   _____

   _____   _____

   _____   _____

3) _____   _____

   _____   _____

   _____   _____

What are the positives of owning sadness?

☐ Relief

☐ Being less controlled

☐ Greater physical health

☐ Not hiding pain

☐ Being more honest

☐ Other

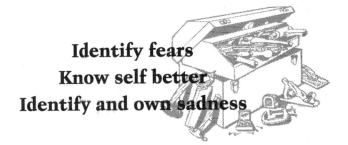

**Identify fears
Know self better
Identify and own sadness**

Today, I am grateful for _____

Angry? Me?

If anger is a feeling you know well, skip this section and focus on sadness, fear, and guilt. Intense anger often indicates that other feelings are hidden — covered by the anger.

For many addicts, anger avoidance is a key issue. We have learned from an early age to quickly diffuse our anger to avoid negative consequences. We have internalized this model and as adults avoid anger to keep ourselves safe. We avoid anger because anger may have a variety of emotional issues attached to it. We may have had a parent who was consistently forceful with their anger. We now want to avoid expressing our own anger so as not to be like our parent. We may have a variety of personal beliefs that preclude us from expressing anger.

> Healthy people don't get angry
> I will be shamed and blamed by others
> Being angry means losing control

Expressing Anger

Many times we have no awareness of our anger. We may be frightened of our anger, or frightened of other people's anger, or we may have so much anger we feel explosive. If you have difficulty expressing anger, it is important to explore how you perceive your anger. Complete the following sentences.

When I am angry, I

_____

_____

_____

When I am angry, I feel

_____

_____

_____

If people see me angry, I feel

_____

_____

_____

When people get angry, I

_____

_____

_____

If you were unable to complete the previous exercise because you are never angry, complete the following statements.

I'm never angry because

_____

_____

_____

If I ever got angry, I'd

_____

_____

_____

I might have felt better if I'd gotten angry when

_____

_____

_____

Complete the following sentence.

When I was a child or teenager, I can remember being angry about… (whether or not anyone else knew that you were angry):

1) _____

2) _____

3) _____

If you have difficulty identifying your anger, you may want to think in terms of the words "frustrated," "disgusted," "irritated," or "upset about." If that helps, go back to the previous exercise and try it again, only with your new words.

Potential Anger

If you still have difficulty identifying your anger, try thinking of five things that took place in your childhood and adolescence that you could have been angry about. You may not have gotten angry or frustrated, but the situation was frustrating and the potential anger was there. Another way of looking at it is to imagine a young child at age five, seven, nine, etc., and put him/her in your family in the same situation. Make a list of what this child could be angry about.

1) _____

2) _____

3) _____

4) _____

5) _____

Check the behaviors that describe what you did as a child when you were angry:

☐ Pouted

☐ Screamed (at whom?)

☐ Was sarcastic

☐ Told the person with whom I was angry directly about my anger

☐ Hit harder on the ball field (or other sport)

☐ Ate to stuff my anger

☐ Ran away

☐ Other (fill in) _____

☐ Other (fill in) _____

When I was angry, my mom usually

☐ Never noticed

☐ Noticed, but ignored it

☐ Made me feel embarrassed or ashamed

☐ Made me feel better

☐ Other (fill in) _____

When I felt angry, my dad usually

☐ Never noticed

☐ Noticed, but ignored it

☐ Made me feel embarrassed or ashamed

☐ Made me feel better

☐ Other (fill in) _____

If there was a particular person — a brother, sister or other significant person in your life — that responded to your anger (either negatively or positively), describe how they responded.

_____

_____

_____

Anger Today

Identify present-day anger. On the right-hand side of the page, list people with whom you have shared the specific anger with or you are willing to share that anger with now.

Today I feel angry about: Name

1) _____   _____

   _____   _____

   _____   _____

2) _____   _____

   _____   _____

   _____   _____

3) _____   _____

   _____   _____

   _____   _____

What are the positives of owning anger?

☐ Relief

☐ Being less controlled

☐ Greater physical health

☐ Not hiding pain

☐ Being more honest

☐ Other _____

Identify fear
Identify and own anger
Know self better

Today, I am grateful for _____

Aristotle's Challenge

Anyone can become angry . . . that is easy. But to be angry with the right person, to the right degree, at the right time for the purpose, and in the right way, that is not so easy.
—Aristotle's Challenge

When angry, count to ten before speaking out; if very angry, count to one hundred.
—Thomas Jefferson

Check the statement that best describes the relationship between your anger and your addictive behavior.

☐ I act out (use) because I want to let my anger out

☐ I act out (use) because I want my anger to go away

☐ I act out (use) to get back at others

☐ I act out (use) when I am angry and I don't care about anything

☐ I act out (use) to hurt or punish myself in my anger

Describe in more detail how your anger and your addictive behavior are related.

_____

_____

_____

_____

Unhealthy anger can present itself in a variety of ways.

1) Anger can be overtly expressed with yelling or shaming statements ("You are so stupid, you can't you get anything right!").

2) Anger can be covertly expressed. Anger expressed covertly often is passive aggressive in nature. It may involve procrastinating, being

late, and using sarcasm and making demeaning comments towards others. Family members with unresolved issues between one another may make fun of the other family member. While the content may be delivered in a joking manner, underneath the surface is anger. This is referred to as guerilla humor. We make a hostile remark to somebody with a smile. Should they call us on it, we tell them it was a joke, and often insult them again — asking them why don't they have a "sense of humor."

3) Anger can be retaliatory. This occurs when we find a way to settle the score. Addicts often keep a mental log of who has wronged them and seek ways to get even.

4) Anger can be masked as isolation. "I don't like people, they don't like me and that is just fine. I don't need people." The angry person does not need anything from anybody at any time.

5) Anger can be manifested as depression. Unresolved grief, pain, shame, trauma, and abuse issues can result in tremendous anger, which turned inward is depression. It is much safer and socially acceptable to present a depressed mood to society than an angry mood.

6) Anger, which is a feeling, can move into rage, which is a behavior.

With rage there is no middle ground. We are walking around with a match in one hand and a gas can in the other. So often it is blind rage. All someone has to do is give us the wrong look or not respond as quickly as we like and the next thing we know we are yelling, blaming, accusing, and maybe physically hitting someone. We move from the temperature of one degree to one hundred degrees within seconds.

Check the following ways of anger expression with which you identify.

- ☐ Yelling
- ☐ Shaming statements
- ☐ Being sarcastic
- ☐ Guerilla humor
- ☐ Being late
- ☐ Wanting or needing to "settle the score"

☐ Avoiding anger

☐ Isolation

☐ Depression

☐ Raging behavior(s)

Anger clouds judgment; harms relationships; can lead to violence; and it encourages relapse.

How have you been hurtful to others in the expression of your anger? (Be specific)

Example: It was (is) hurtful to (name) when I

It was (is) hurtful to _____ when I _____

It was (is) hurtful to _____ when I _____

It was (is) hurtful to _____ when I _____

It was (is) hurtful to _____ when I _____

It was (is) hurtful to _____ when I _____

It was (is) hurtful to _____ when I _____

It was (is) hurtful to _____ when I _____

It was (is) hurtful to _____ when I _____

How have you been hurtful to yourself in the expression of your anger?

I hurt myself by _____

I hurt myself by _____

I hurt myself by _____

I hurt myself by _____

I hurt myself by _____

I hurt myself by _____

I hurt myself by _____

I hurt myself by _____

Anger Sentence Stems

Our formative years strongly influenced the way we express our feelings today. The following exercise may offer you some valuable insight. Think back on when you were growing up and complete the following sentences.

When my dad got angry he _____

When my dad got angry he _____

When my dad got angry I _____

When my dad got angry I _____

When my mom got angry she _____

When my mom got angry she _____

When my mom got angry I _____

When my mom got angry I _____

When I got angry at my mom she _____

When I got angry at my mom she _____

When I got angry at my dad he _____

When I got angry at my dad he _____

Today when I get angry I _____

Today when I get angry I _____

There can be a great gap between learning about anger and no longer being hurtful in your anger. These few exercises are meant for you to recognize the possible significance of anger in your recovery. The greater the significance anger plays in your life, the more I encourage you to seek feedback in your recovery group, with a counselor/therapist, or an anger management class. There is no need to be ashamed. Be honest with yourself, not judgmental.

Identify how anger relates to use of addictive substance or process

Identify personal anger expression

Own negative consequences to anger

Recognize generational anger history

Today, I am grateful for _____

Mad . . . and It's Not About You

It is not uncommon for people to use their anger as an excuse to engage in their addiction.

Tim comes home from work agitated and feeling anxious, but he isn't sure why. He has not gambled in four weeks, deliberately staying away from his gambling sites—the horse races and sports bars. He has been feeling depressed and has withdrawn; not sharing his concerns or fears.

As he walks through the door, his teenage daughter races out, telling him she is going out with her boyfriend and will be back late. Tim hates her boyfriend. He rummages through the kitchen, hungry, wondering why his wife and other daughter are not at home. He notices the blinking light on the answering machine, listens to the message, and hears his wife say she is at her sister's for the weekend and his other daughter is spending the night with a friend.

That does it! He doesn't need her and his kids obviously don't need him. So why is he depriving himself? He grabs the car keys, slams the door as he leaves the house, and peels rubber as he heads down the road to the local sports bar.

Tim may have legitimate reasons to be frustrated about his relationship with his wife and daughters, but his need to gamble is so great he uses his righteous sense of anger as an excuse.

Identify situations in your life when you used anger as a vehicle that would allow you to resume your addictive behavior.

1) _____

2) _____

3) _____

4) _____

**Recognize using anger
to empower the addiction**

Today, I am grateful for _____

 # Hostility Roadmap

Identify the last three situations that made you angry.

1) _____

_____

_____

2) _____

_____

_____

3) _____

_____

_____

How did you respond in these situations?

1) _____

_____

2) _____

_____

3) _____

_____

Now look at the Hostility Road Map that follows to see how to effectively respond.

HOSTILITY ROADMAP WITH STRATEGIES

My Cynical Thought . . . Angry Feeling . . . or Aggressive Action

Is the matter worth my continued attention?

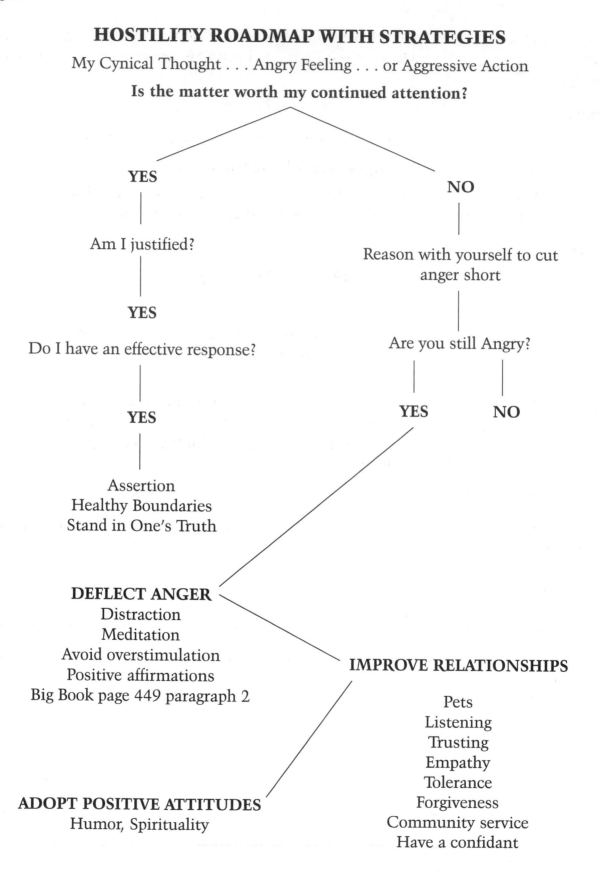

YES

Am I justified?

YES

Do I have an effective response?

YES

Assertion
Healthy Boundaries
Stand in One's Truth

NO

Reason with yourself to cut
anger short

Are you still Angry?

YES   **NO**

DEFLECT ANGER
Distraction
Meditation
Avoid overstimulation
Positive affirmations
Big Book page 449 paragraph 2

IMPROVE RELATIONSHIPS

Pets
Listening
Trusting
Empathy
Tolerance
Forgiveness
Community service
Have a confidant

ADOPT POSITIVE ATTITUDES
Humor, Spirituality

Below are examples of situations that might anger us and cause us to respond in a hostile manner. Using the tools provided in the Hostility Roadmap, see how effective responses were developed.

Example:

> Another driver cuts me off on my way to work and I am infuriated.
>
> **Is the matter worth my continued attention?** No.
>
> **Reason with yourself to cut anger short**. "He didn't see me." "I am nervous about my meeting today at work and I am over-reacting."

Example:

> I am angry at my 17 year old for wrecking my car.
>
> **Am I justified?** Yes.
>
> **Do I have an effective response?** No. "I want to say, you stupid so and so, I can't trust you with anything." Reason with yourself to cut anger short.
>
> **Response is:** "I wrecked my dad's car when I was fourteen. He didn't take time to even drive with me and I thought it was funny. Maybe I need to take more time with my son in the car, for the sake of spending time, not just driving."
>
> **Are you still angry?** No. "Not so much."

Now look at the three situations that made you angry and develop your own Roadmap for your responses.

Situation 1

_____

_____

_____

Situation 2

_____

_____

_____

Situation 3

_____

_____

_____

_____

Evaluate justification for anger
Identify effective responses

Today, I am grateful for _____

Whose Poison Is It?

Resentments are like burrs in our saddle blanket: if we do not get rid of them, they fester into an infection. James, who is nine months sober, is working in a real estate office for an employer who is twelve years sober. James relapses and enters treatment. When he returns to work, he feels misunderstood because he was not welcomed back with open arms. In his hurt and confusion, he jumps to anger and resentment. He finds another job and he stops attending Twelve Step meetings. If he sees his former boss, he makes an effort to avoid him. When asked why he is so resentful, all he can say is that his former boss is a jerk.

Karen, new to recovery for her anorexia, is resentful towards her sister whom she believes is also anorexic and not seeking recovery.

Tim, a sex addict, is immediately resentful when his wife rejects his sexual advances and uses his resentment to fuel acting out.

In *The Sermon on the Mount*, Emmet Fox describes resentment as the equivalent of swallowing poison in the hope it will kill the person who is the target of our anger.

On page 449 in the *Big Book of Alcoholics Anonymous*, Dr. Paul O. writes:

> "And acceptance is the answer to *all* my problems today. When I am disturbed, it is because I find some person, place, thing, or situation — some fact of my life —unacceptable to me, and I find no serenity until I accept that person, place, thing, or situation as being exactly the way it is supposed to be at this moment. Nothing, absolutely nothing, happens in God's world by mistake. Until I could accept my alcoholism, I could not stay sober; unless I accept life completely on life's terms, I cannot be happy. I need to concentrate not so much on what needs to be changed in the world as on what needs to be changed in me and in my attitudes. Shakespeare said, 'All the world's a stage, all the men and women merely players.' He forgot to mention that I was the chief critic. I was always able to see the flaw in every person, every situation. And, I was always glad to point it out..."

What does this passage say to you?

_____

_____

_____

What does it mean for you to hang on to resentments?

_____

_____

_____

What would it mean to accept that you have been hurt or wronged and that you can no longer change that?

_____

_____

_____

What does it mean to take responsibility for your own feelings?

_____

_____

_____

Ultimately, who pays the price for hanging on to resentments?

_____

_____

_____

Today, are you willing to let go of your resentments?

☐ Yes   ☐ No

In *As Bill Sees It, The AA Way of Life,* Bill W. wrote:

> "Resentment is the Number One offender. It destroys more alcoholics than anything else. From it stem all forms of spiritual disease, for we have been not only mentally and physically ill, we have also been spiritually ill. When our spiritual malady is overcome, we straighten out mentally and physically."

> "In dealing with our resentments, we set them on paper. We listed people, institutions, or principles with whom we were angry. We asked ourselves why we were angry. In most cases it was found that our self esteem, our pocketbooks, our ambitions, our personal relationships (including sex) were hurt or threatened." He would go on to say "The most heated bit of letter writing can be a wonderful safety valve — providing the wastebasket is somewhere nearby." (Page 39, Dealing With Resentments)

> "Few people have been more victimized by resentments than have we alcoholics. A burst of temper could spoil a day, and a well-nursed grudge could make us miserably ineffective. Nor were we ever skillful in separating justified from unjustified anger. As we saw it, our wrath was always justified. Anger, that occasional luxury of more balanced people, could keep us on an emotional jag indefinitely. These 'dry benders' often led straight to the bottle." (Page 179, Coping With Anger)

If we maintain our resentments, we find that we want support in our misery and seek out people who will provide that. Unfortunately they are usually not others in recovery. It is often our previous using friends who are most apt to support us in our chronic negative attitude.

Resentments are experienced when we feel discounted, slighted or unheard. Many times the person we are feeling slighted by is totally unaware of the behavior we interpreted as a personal insult. Resentments are often built on assumptions. "When you don't look at me, I assume you think you are better than me." "When you don't include me in a social gathering, I assume you think that I am not good enough."

Resentments are built on entitlement, which are a form of unrealistic expectations and impatience. "I have been sober six weeks now. I resent the fact that my wife still doesn't trust me." "Because I am changing, I feel that I should be rewarded." "Now that I am sober, my boss should give me that promotion I deserve." "Somebody owes me."

An equation that may be helpful to remember is — unrealistic expectations + impatience = resentments.

Resentments

The following exercise will help to identify how resentments may be present in your life.

Examples might be:

> I resent that I am an addict
>
> I resent that in recovery I can't live like I used to
>
> I resent the guy who sits next to me in meetings. He just looks like he thinks he is better than me
>
> I resent all the amends I need to make for my past behaviors

I am resentful that _____

I am resentful that _____

I am resentful that _____

I am resentful that _____

I am resentful that _____

One of the ways to move from resentment is to ask, what is the resentment covering? Are resentment and anger covering up another feeling? An example of this would be resenting the amends process that we as addicts need to engage in. In truth, we may be fearful of the feelings that could come up from making amends. We are scared silly, we feel guilty.

This resentment could be reframed as, "I am afraid of my feelings when making amends to others. I feel guilty and I am scared."

Resentments are also about control. Resenting others is often about resenting those who you believe will interfere with your plans. If this could be true for you, refer back to Control section.

Different ways to move away from a place of resentment are:

> When assuming, check it out
>
> Put yourself in somebody else's shoes—it may allow expectations to be more realistic
>
> Identify and own the feelings the resentment is covering
>
> Be willing to live and let live

From the resentments you listed, explore ways to move away from that place of resentment.

My resentment is:

_____

_____

_____

Different ways I can move from my place of resentment are:

_____

_____

_____

My resentment is:

_____

_____

_____

Different ways I can move from my place of resentment are:

_____

_____

_____

My resentment is:

_____

_____

_____

Different ways I can move from my place of resentment are:

_____

_____

_____

Twelve Step work is vital to addressing resentments. Specifically, Steps Four, Five, Eight, and Nine are related to amends and resentments.

Have you done Steps Four, Five, Eight, and Nine?

☐ Yes   ☐ No

If so, how was your experience working these Steps?

_____

_____

_____

This is a good time to review them and see if you have left anything out.

If you haven't done these Steps, what has gotten in the way of doing them?

_____

_____

_____

Do you have a home group?

☐ Yes   ☐ No

Do you have a sponsor?

☐ Yes   ☐ No

Now that you have completed these questions, please refer to page 66 of the Big Book and the discussion of resentments. It speaks to how the resentful person has concluded that the world and its people were often quite wrong. It says,

"To conclude that others were wrong was as far as most of us ever got. The usual outcome was that people continued to wrong us and we stayed sore. Sometimes it was remorse and then we were sore at ourselves. But the more we fought and tried to have our own way, the worse matters got. As in war, the victor only seemed to win. Our moments of triumph were short lived."

"It is plain that a life, which includes deep resentment, leads only to futility and unhappiness. To the precise extent that we permit these, do we squander the hours that might have been worthwhile. But with the alcoholic, whose hope is the maintenance and growth of a spiritual experience, this business of resentment is infinitely grave. We found that it is fatal. For when harboring such feelings we shut ourselves off from the sunlight of the Spirit. The insanity of alcohol returns and we drink again. With us, to drink is to die."

While this is spoken to the alcoholic, it has just as much meaning irrespective of the nature of the addiction. Each day we need to be aware of how resentments are present in our lives and to act on them constructively and immediately.

Understand danger of resentments
Identify resentments
Identify behavior that prevents resentments

Today, I am grateful for _____

The Needle is in the Red Zone

As addicts, we often hang on to resentments. As part of a program of recovery, it is essential to learn as much about our resentments as we can. In order to learn how to release resentments, we need to first know the specific themes of our resentments and how they are present in our lives.

Having listed specific resentments in a previous exercise, do you see any particular themes to your resentments? Are they regarding specific people or issues?

_____

_____

_____

Resentments often stem from unrealistic expectations or distorted thinking. When we are resentful, we often lose our serenity and in our anger have a **SLIP**. This stands for **S**obriety **L**osing **I**ts **P**riority.

The following exercise is designed to help you identify resentments, the thinking associated with resentments, and the consequences. Example:

I am resentful at	For	What I told myself that was unrealistic or distorted	What I did
My co-worker	Not including me in a project	He didn't value my work; I'm not good enough	I got loaded
My spouse	Having friends	I should have all of my wife's attention whenever I want it	I had affairs
My sponsor	Spending time with others	I should have all of my sponsor's attention	I didn't follow directions

I am resentful at	For	What I told myself that was unrealistic or distorted	What I did

Looking back at the resentments you listed, what role did you have in the situation(s) that led to your resentments?

Example:

> Co-workers—I made assumption
> My spouse—I had unrealistic expectations
> My sponsor—I had unrealistic expectations, grandiose thinking

_____

_____

_____

_____

_____

_____

_____

If resentments are a problem for you, it may be helpful to do a daily inventory of resentments and identify your role. We can only be accountable for ourselves. Remember, it's our poison, not theirs.

Today I will let go of _____

Today, I will surrender it to my Higher Power.

Today I will let go of _____

Today, I will surrender it to my Higher Power.

Today I will let go of _____

Today, I will surrender it to my Higher Power.

Identifying resentments and then surrendering them to your Higher Power will be extremely helpful. Remember that this exercise is to help you release expectations and resentments. Each day as you learn to release expectations, fears, and resentments, you learn to live life guided by your Higher Power.

Be accountable
Own responsibility
Let go

Today, I am grateful for _____

One, Two, Buckle My Shoe— Three Four . . .

To begin our journey in recovery, we need to address our primary addiction(s) first. These are the addictions that are the most potentially life-threatening to us. Today it is more common than ever for people to be addicted to more than one behavior, substance or process, but only one addiction is initially identified. Another curious cycle happens for many addicts in early recovery: our addictive tendencies begin to search for new areas of our lives to present themselves. As addicts, we are often compulsive people. Just because we begin recovery doesn't mean we stop being compulsive. The disease process begins to seek imbalance in areas of our lives that were never problematic before. Perhaps we begin to work longer and longer hours, begin to exercise compulsively, start or increase smoking, or adopt a variety of other addictive behaviors. So often the disease will not rest until it has re-established a hold in some other area(s) of our lives. It is extremely important to be aware of this cycle because these new areas of imbalance not only become addictions themselves, but also often trigger a relapse of our primary addiction(s).

Many times we experience shame regarding underlying addictions and want to keep them a secret. In the Twelve Step programs there is a saying: "We are only as sick as our secret." The more secrets we keep, the more shame we experience, which fuels the addictive process and may lead to relapse.

John told this story regarding multiple addictions:

> "I began recovery for my drinking three years ago. I got a sponsor, prayed, meditated, and attended lots of meetings. I figured that doing these things would guarantee me ongoing sobriety, *One Day at a Time*. What I didn't know was that under the surface I had another addiction — sex addiction.

> "My pattern usually looked like this. Several times a week, I would have a few drinks after work at a local bar. Usually by 7 o'clock each night I had struck up a conversation with someone at the bar. At least once a week, I had sex with one of these people I had met at the bar. When I began recovery around my drinking, I figured that I had been having anonymous sex just because I was drunk and lonely. I was wrong. Even though I was going to my Alcoholics Anonymous meetings, I found myself missing this anonymous sex more and more. I began to fantasize about having sex with strangers. I felt a great deal of shame about this and kept this

whole area of my life secret from my sponsor and others in the program. I thought that they would think less of me or judge me. I told myself that I could control my behavior. I thought that maybe I could go back to my local bar and just drink club soda. Maybe I could just have conversations and not go home with one of these strangers.

"Before I knew it, I was back on my familiar barstool several times per week — cruising. I began going home with strangers, but it was much harder for me now because without the alcohol I wasn't the smooth talker. That was when I relapsed with my drinking. The first night I felt terrible, but ignored my feelings by having sex with a stranger. Very soon, I was drinking more than before and having anonymous sex almost every night of the week. Now I see that underneath my addiction to alcohol was also an addiction to sex. I had deluded myself into believing that I was only a drunk and ignored my addiction to sex. By doing this, my sex addiction led me to relapse with alcohol. Today I attend Alcoholics Anonymous and Sex Addicts Anonymous. I know that I need to be on the lookout for how, when, and where other addictions may present themselves in my life."

Jim was extremely distraught about the consequences of his gambling. He had no doubt he was an addict. Every aspect of his life was negatively affected. One day, after a failed suicide attempt, he sought treatment. While he was no longer deluded in his thinking about the role gambling played in his life, and was sincere about wanting to stop, in four months he had relapsed three times. Each relapse was longer than the previous and had more dire consequences. Each relapse was precipitated by his use of alcohol. He had been told to stop drinking to help his recovery. What he only now recognized was that while he was further along in the progression of his gambling, he engaged in both gambling and drinking addictively. They were interactive, a package, and recovery from both would be necessary.

Lynn began to address her eating disorder — a cycle of compulsive overeating and then starving — only after developing health problems that she could not ignore. She discovered she acted out sexually in tandem with her starving and was sexually avoidant in her overeating phase. Addressing the relationship of the two addictions was essential in order to garner recovery. Her eating disorder and her addictive sexual behavior existed in tandem with each other.

If you are an alcoholic, are you still using other drugs such as marijuana, cocaine, or prescription medication (without the complete knowledge of your physician, sponsor and counselor)?

☐ Yes   ☐ No

If you are recovering from drugs, are you still using alcohol?

☐ Yes ☐ No

The following is a list of extremely common addictions:

Alcohol
Other Drugs
Gambling
Spending
Risk—high risk sports, business ventures, dangerous activities
Sex
Relationships
Work
Exercise
Food Related Behaviors
Compulsive Overeating
Binge Eating
Starving
Purging (via exercise, laxatives, vomiting, etc.)

Have you ever wondered whether or not any of these were problematic for you?

☐ Yes ☐ No

Has anyone ever suggested that any of these could be problematic?

☐ Yes ☐ No

Have you used any of these to medicate your feelings?

☐ Yes ☐ No

Do you engage in any of these to garner feelings?

☐ Yes ☐ No

Have you engaged in any of these and then made efforts to lessen or stop the behavior only to resume the behavior?

☐ Yes ☐ No

Have you experienced financial, health, relationship or family problems as a result?

☐ Yes ☐ No

Would it be wise to seek an outside opinion as to whether or not your recovery is threatened by your involvement in any of the above?

☐ Yes   ☐ No

What are you feeling as you answer these questions?

_____

_____

_____

If you believe that there may be additional addictions, an immediate plan of treatment must go into effect.

- If you have a sponsor, talk to this person about developing a plan of action.

- Find a Twelve Step program most appropriate to the addiction.

- Find an inpatient or outpatient treatment facility to address the addiction(s).

Able to identify and own multi-addictions

Today, I am grateful for _____

Triggers—and I don't mean the horse

Triggers are specific memories, situations, and behaviors that jeopardize recovery. Pulling the trigger on a gun signals that a bullet is about to be fired. For the addict, triggers bring them closer to relapse.

John, a recovering sex addict and alcoholic, describes his relapse. "Even though I had quit drinking and acting out sexually, I still spent a lot of time in bars. Most of my business meetings were held there because that is where my clients preferred to meet. It became harder and harder for me not to order a drink or talk to attractive women. Finally one night, I gave in and ordered a drink. The next thing I remember was being at a motel with someone I didn't even know." For John, a significant trigger to re-engage in his addictive behaviors was the environment in which he spent time. His addictive thinking led him to believe that he was *"strong enough"* to resist his environment.

Triggers differ for each addict. One particularly strong trigger is euphoric recall. This is when we romanticize using behaviors and forget about the negative consequences.

Susan, a compulsive over spender said, "When I first got into recovery, I spent a lot of time thinking about my spending sprees. I used to focus on one particular memory where I went on a $3,000 shopping trip to buy an entire new wardrobe. The more I thought about that spending spree, the more beautiful the clothes and I became and I was tempted to go back out and start spending again. What I forgot about that $3,000 shopping trip was that it was the trip that sent me into bankruptcy."

When you talk about your active addiction, do you tend to focus predominantly on the pleasurable or exciting times?

☐ Yes   ☐ No

Do you tend to romanticize various using experiences?

☐ Yes   ☐ No

If we continue to do this, the addict in us will begin to remind us of how nice it might be to go back out "just one more time" and engage in our addictive behaviors again. After all, how bad could it be? We are in recovery now, right? If we just had a few drinks, just had an affair, just whatever, we would be able to stop if we wanted to, wouldn't we?

The answer is **NO**. Once we went back out, our lives would quickly disintegrate into the old madness of our addictions. This is how we, as addicts, work. More is always better. We want to do everything to the extreme.

In the last month, have you experienced euphoric recall?

☐ Yes   ☐ No

In the last week, have you experienced euphoric recall?

☐ Yes   ☐ No

Identify how you engage in euphoric recall. With each, note the negative consequences to the idealized memory. Examples:

Euphoric Recall	Negative Consequences
Hours spent in bar with friends	Two drinking and driving arrests
Thrill in throwing the dice; making my point	Eventually I was the loser
I saw myself looking good	I was a walking skeleton

If we find ourselves falling into euphoric recall, there are several important steps we can take:

- Immediately disengage from fantasizing and/or leave the situation.

- Call your sponsor. He or she will know what you are going through; they have been there themselves.

- Call someone on your Twelve Step meeting list. Reaching out to another addict can be a lifeline.

- Go to a meeting. Being able to share your experiences with other addicts helps you to remember why you are in recovery.

Many of the above suggestions come directly from the Emergency Plan. That is why it is important to have it with you at all times. You never know when it will be needed. Remember that the hardest day in recovery is always better than the best day out using.

Smell and taste can be triggers. The smell of beer or whiskey could be a trigger. The taste can be a trigger. This is why it is dangerous territory to drink "near beers" or non-alcoholic beers or wine.

Social stressors can be significant triggers for relapse. There may have been many situations — going to work, going on dates, to family picnics — where you medicated yourself with your addiction of choice beforehand. Now, in sobriety, these same situations present themselves. When you start to feel pressured and uncomfortable, the urge to return to the addiction(s) can feel overwhelming.

Other triggers can include loss of relationships and death. Maybe your relationship has recently broken up or someone close to you has passed away. In your addictions you would not have felt the pain because you would have been numb. Now, maybe for the first time, this pain is present and you choose to face it sober.

Are certain feelings triggers for you?

☐ Yes   ☐ No

Assess Potential Triggers

It is important to learn to assess for potential high-risk situations and triggers to relapse.

Complete the following exercise:

Name triggers you are aware of	Identify action to lessen or remove exposure to trigger
1)	
2)	
3)	
4)	
5)	

One area that most addicts find particularly difficult is the amount of excess time present in recovery. Often, hours or days would be spent each week engaging in addictive behaviors. Now, in recovery, it feels as though there is a void.

Are there areas of your life you feel are empty now that you are in recovery?

1) _____

_____

2) _____

_____

3) _____

_____

What positive recovery activities can you now engage in to account for the extra time in your life?

1) _____

_____

2) _____

_____

3) _____

_____

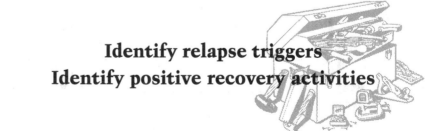

Identify relapse triggers
Identify positive recovery activities

Today, I am grateful for _____

The Helping Hand

As addicts, we have all had enablers in our life — people who, out of their care and love for us, "help" us in a manner that makes it easier to not feel the consequences of our behavior. Enablers buffer us from our addiction(s), helping the addiction to prevail.

- Marie is a compulsive gambler. Her parents pay her credit card bills so she won't have bad credit.

- Carole's husband seeks help from friends in the police department to reduce her drug charges.

- Cindy's mom and dad demand she switch schools when the athletic director tells them their daughter's fractures are related to an eating disorder.

- Charlie's dad buys him new cars and pays his college tuition in spite of the fact that Charlie can't keep a job, wrecks his cars, and drops his classes mid-term.

- Richard's wife ignores the phone calls from his many girlfriends, wondering why these women are trying to be so hurtful to her and her husband.

None of these caring people hold the addict accountable for their behavior.

Identify your enablers and their enabling behavior.

Name _____

1) _____

2) _____

3) _____

4) _____

Name _____

1) _____

2) _____

3) _____

4) _____

Name _____

1) _____

2) _____

3) _____

4) _____

Name _____

1) _____

2) _____

3) _____

4) _____

As the addict, we need to learn to ask others to not assume responsibility for our behaviors. We need to meet our own wants and needs. A part of our recovery is being responsible and accountable for our actions. If feasible, approach your enablers and tell them their behavior (be specific) is not helping you and is getting in the way of your recovery. While others have probably told them this, they are more likely to believe it when they hear it directly from you. Take responsibility for whether or not you allow others to enable you.

Name your enablers again:

Name _____

Are you willing to quit relying on this person to enable you?

☐ Yes   ☐ No

Name _____

Are you willing to quit relying on this person to enable you?

☐ Yes   ☐ No

Name _____

Are you willing to quit relying on this person to enable you?

☐ Yes   ☐ No

Name _____

Are you willing to quit relying on this person to enable you?

☐ Yes   ☐ No

We alone are accountable for our behavior, bringing us face to face with the reality that recovery is about showing up and taking responsibility.

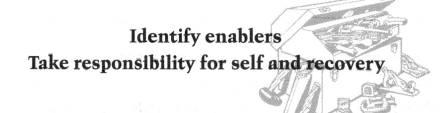

**Identify enablers
Take responsibility for self and recovery**

Today, I am grateful for _____

Trigger Relationships

Certain behaviors within relationships are serious relapse triggers. For Mike, working and traveling with his alcoholic father is a serious trigger for his recovery from substance abuse. "It is extremely difficult for me to work and be around my father when he is actively engaging in his addiction. I am constantly confronted by my anger with him and my own desire to use."

For Lori, a sex addict, being around her brother-in-law, with whom she acted out sexually, is a trigger. Also, being around her sister, with whom she has tremendous guilt, is a trigger. "I feel so much shame and guilt when I am around them. I constantly think about my actions and beat myself up. The hard thing is that I can't avoid them because they are part of my family."

For Kevin, returning to work where his co-workers and friends use drugs is a trigger. "How am I supposed to go back to work with these people? My whole social life with them is centered on drinking and using. We would use at lunch, after work, and weekends. Without chemicals, how do I relate to these people?"

For Sherry, being around her father, who was her childhood perpetrator, triggers her eating disorders. "Whenever I see my dad, I feel so much anger, pain, and shame, I medicate my feelings by eating. Then, I feel guilty for acting out in my eating disorder. It is a vicious cycle."

It is vital that you identify the relationships that will be significant triggers.

Which people are the greatest triggers in your life?

1) _____

2) _____

3) _____

What is it about your relationship with them that is a trigger for you?

1) _____

2) _____

3) _____

When thinking of these trigger relationships, consider:

- Do you need to say some things directly to this person to set the stage for a different relationship?

- In what ways can you limit contact?

- What acts of self-care can you employ if you must see this person? Acts of self-care could be things you do before and after you have seen them, as well as what you do and say while with them. For example, you may talk to your sponsor prior to a visit. If this is a family reunion, you may choose to stay away from where so many others are staying and partying, and also limit the amount of time you spend at the event. Another limit to employ when focusing on self-care is to know ahead of time what topics of conversation you are or are not willing to have.

- Would Al-Anon be a useful support? Al-Anon is a Twelve Step self-help group for families and friends of addicts.

- List other strategies that would be helpful.

- Talk to others in recovery about their successful strategies.

Recent Relationships

Allowing ourselves to be in painful relationships where we do not take care of ourselves is also a trigger. Sue, who is new to recovery from her eating disorder but doesn't address how her partner chronically berates her, is very likely to relapse.

Name two people with whom you have had a recent painful relationship:

1) _____

2) _____

Think about the most recent relationship and answer these questions:

What hurtful behavior took place that you tolerated?

_____

_____

_____

What rationalizations did you use to accept the hurtful behavior and allow it to continue?

_____

_____

_____

In what ways did you take care of yourself?

_____

_____

_____

In what ways did you *not* take care of yourself?

_____

_____

_____

How were you hurtful toward the other person in the relationship?

_____

_____

_____

Repeat the same questions in regards to the second person who is a trigger for you.

What hurtful behavior took place that you tolerated?

_____

_____

What rationalizations did you use to accept the hurtful behavior and allow it to continue?

_____

_____

_____

In what ways did you take care of yourself?

_____

_____

_____

In what ways did you *not* take care of yourself?

_____

_____

_____

How were you hurtful toward the other person in the relationship?

_____

_____

_____

Identify any patterns or similarities between these two lists.

_____

_____

_____

It is essential to identify the aspects of relationships that can be hurtful to your recovery. While we will not always be able to stop others from hurtful behavior, we are responsible for how we react.

**Identify trigger relationships
Plan for self-care**

Today, I am grateful for _____

Relationship View

We have gone through much of our lives making assumptions or guessing about what is normal or what is appropriate in relationships. Because of a lack of healthy models, we are frequently operating in a vacuum. The following characteristics offer a healthier framework for a relationship.

Respect

My respect is an acceptance of who you are, your autonomy, the uniqueness of you. Respect is an attitude for which courtesy is an expression.

Honesty

Honesty and open communication mean that people are free to be themselves. "I have given up fear of rejection when I am less than perfect, when I am vulnerable, when it may mean you disagree with me. I can tell you my feelings, my thoughts, without fear of a major catastrophe."

Realistic Expectations

We need to be realistic about what we can offer others and what they can offer us. A history of growing up with enmeshed boundaries, having unrealistic expectations placed on us, or even magical thinking on our part, can cause us to have very unrealistic expectations of others and ourselves. Be aware that other people are not going to be available to meet all of our needs. Nor should they. We are responsible for many of our needs, while different people together (friends, family and partner) meet varying interpersonal needs. We must be cautious of any one person trying to meet **all** of our needs at **all** times. It is likely that person is very fearful of rejection, won't take responsibility for themselves, and hasn't developed a sense of self.

Trust

Trust means, "I feel psychologically and physically safe with you. I have neither fears nor anxieties with respect to your treatment of me." For there to be trust, there needs to be consistency, predictability, and a demonstrated reliability that a person will follow through with their intentions. Trust is like a brick wall. It takes time to build and develop.

Autonomy

Intimacy is a sharing of autonomy. Real autonomy means each of us takes full responsibility for our own lives, for evolving into the best human being we can be. We fulfill our own life scripts and exercise our own physical, emotional, and spiritual energies. With autonomy we have the ability to be clear about our own needs, while being respectful to the boundaries and limits of others. We are also able to honor the other person's differences.

We need to be cautious, as autonomy sometimes passes for unbridled, unmitigated selfishness. "To hell with the rest of the world, I am going to get what I want when I want it because I am entitled to do what I please." That is not true. No one is entitled to get what he wants when he wants it from anyone. That is selfish, intrusive, and greedy.

While a healthy relationship is not a power struggle between two rigidly autonomous beings, neither should it be symbiotic. The two of you do not have to think and feel the same way about all things. We want to share ourselves without collapsing into one being. A healthy relationship is autonomy that grows in strength when shared.

Shared Power

A healthy relationship is about shared power, not control. Both people in the relationship are able to take initiative and to respond. They are able to stand side by side. There is a mutual give and take. We relinquish the need to be right. We eliminate the idea of ownership. There is mutuality and reciprocity in the relationship.

The notion of shared power with children is often a problem for parents. However, when children feel powerless, there are usually very negative consequences for both parents and children. While parents do need to operate from a position of authority, and are responsible for providing healthy structure and boundaries, they can, nonetheless, offer children age-appropriate areas of mutual power sharing.

Tenderness

Tenderness is demonstrated with physical affection. This is the kind of nonsexual physical touching we all need to thrive. There is nurturing touch that says, "I am here, you are not alone." "I offer my support." "Hello."

Tenderness is also expressed in words and attitude. After being with people for long periods of time, it is easy to let go of the little niceties we offer to those we don't know as well. Over time, it is easy to take our partners, our parents, and even our friends for granted.

Time

Relationships need time. When 150 couples in committed relationships (living together for over four years) were asked how much time they spent with their partner each day, the average was twenty-three minutes. Twenty-three minutes with the person each considered the most important to his or her life! People grow apart for many reasons, but for some it is as simple as getting caught up in other responsibilities and not taking time to "be" in a relationship. Valued relationships need time.

Long-Term Commitment

To have a healthy relationship we need to pay attention to the relationship's dynamics and make a commitment to working on our part. We trust that if there are problems in our relationship, the two of us will work them out. We trust that when there are problems, it does not mean the relationship is over.

Commitment does not mean you stay in a relationship regardless of what may occur. At times, as people change, relationships are renegotiated and commitments are reinforced or lessened. But, when we make a commitment, we do what we can to make the relationship work; we do not allow ourselves to be abused, nor do we give up our integrity in the process.

Forgiveness

There has to be room for forgiveness in any relationship. Forgiveness does not mean selling your heart, soul, or integrity to have peace. It means remembering and letting go. It is a cleansing of your pain and anger. It means maintaining your integrity while being able to let go.

Charting a Relationship

Using these characteristics, the following is an example of how Tom sees himself relating to his seventeen-year-old son. One means the least, ten means the most.

	X									**Respect**
1	2	3	4	5	6	7	8	9	10	
		X								**Honesty**
1	2	3	4	5	6	7	8	9	10	
		X								**Realistic Expectations**
1	2	3	4	5	6	7	8	9	10	
	X									**Trust**
1	2	3	4	5	6	7	8	9	10	
	X									**Autonomy**
1	2	3	4	5	6	7	8	9	10	
			X							**Shared Power**
1	2	3	4	5	6	7	8	9	10	
			X							**Tenderness**
1	2	3	4	5	6	7	8	9	10	

										Time
			X							
1	2	3	4	5	6	7	8	9	10	

										Long-Term Commitment
							X			
1	2	3	4	5	6	7	8	9	10	

										Forgiveness
			X							
1	2	3	4	5	6	7	8	9	10	

Clearly, this relationship is struggling. It takes a lot of self-honesty to benefit from this, but in doing so, Tom realized he was still angry with his son for not actively pursuing a particular sport, football, and especially angry for his sensitivity and orientation to music. In doing this, Tom realized the crux to establishing a better relationship with his son would be to work on allowing autonomy and respecting his son for his uniqueness and individuality. He recognized he needed to own the loss of never having been the great athlete he wanted to be. He was only now beginning to acknowledge that it was more important to know his son than to hang onto regrets.

Charting Your Relationships

Think of someone with whom you have a significant relationship. On a scale of one to ten, one meaning the least and ten the most, chart the relationship you have chosen to examine.

Name _____

										Respect
1	2	3	4	5	6	7	8	9	10	

										Honesty
1	2	3	4	5	6	7	8	9	10	

										Realistic Expectations
1	2	3	4	5	6	7	8	9	10	

										Trust
1	2	3	4	5	6	7	8	9	10	

										Autonomy
1	2	3	4	5	6	7	8	9	10	

										Shared Power
1	2	3	4	5	6	7	8	9	10	

										Tenderness
1	2	3	4	5	6	7	8	9	10	

										Time
1	2	3	4	5	6	7	8	9	10	

Long-Term Commitment

1	2	3	4	5	6	7	8	9	10

Forgiveness

1	2	3	4	5	6	7	8	9	10

Now that you have completed the exercise, identify short-term, intermediate, and long-range goals for what you can do to improve the relationship.

Short-term goals

1) _____

2) _____

3) _____

Intermediate goals

1) _____

2) _____

3) _____

Long-term goals

1) _____

2) _____

3) _____

Identify healthy criteria for relationships
Be accountable for self in relationships

Today, I am grateful for _____

Watch your step

Imagine pilots preparing a plane for takeoff. They perform a rigorous examination of the plane and go through a checklist before each flight to ensure their safety. Should anything problematic be found, they have specific procedures to address the situation. Recovery is much the same. By having a warning signs checklist, we are able to monitor if any addictive behaviors, patterns, or signs of relapse are occurring. Sponsors and significant others can also be an excellent source of feedback in helping to monitor this behavior. This does not mean they are responsible for our recovery. It means that perhaps they have a more objective approach and can see things in our behavior that we are unable to.

Warning Signs Checklist

The Warning Signs Checklist will help to monitor your behavior. Should problematic behaviors start to occur, you will have a specific plan of how to address the warning signs.

Fill out the following warning signs checklist, circling the number that applies. On a scale of one to ten, one means you least identify with the statement, ten means you most identify.

I have no interest in doing things	1	2	3	4	5	6	7	8	9	10
I have no interest in my appearance	1	2	3	4	5	6	7	8	9	10
I am discouraged about the future	1	2	3	4	5	6	7	8	9	10
I have trouble sleeping	1	2	3	4	5	6	7	8	9	10
I rarely see my friends	1	2	3	4	5	6	7	8	9	10
I rarely go to Twelve Step meetings	1	2	3	4	5	6	7	8	9	10
I rarely see my sponsor	1	2	3	4	5	6	7	8	9	10
I eat very little	1	2	3	4	5	6	7	8	9	10
I am distant from my family/friends	1	2	3	4	5	6	7	8	9	10
I don't enjoy activities	1	2	3	4	5	6	7	8	9	10
I believe I could use or engage in addictive behavior to some degree	1	2	3	4	5	6	7	8	9	10
I believe I can control my addiction	1	2	3	4	5	6	7	8	9	10
I am very aggressive	1	2	3	4	5	6	7	8	9	10
I feel like I need to control things	1	2	3	4	5	6	7	8	9	10
I don't like to listen to others	1	2	3	4	5	6	7	8	9	10
I feel resentful	1	2	3	4	5	6	7	8	9	10
My relationships are toxic	1	2	3	4	5	6	7	8	9	10
I have lots of secrets	1	2	3	4	5	6	7	8	9	10
I feel ashamed	1	2	3	4	5	6	7	8	9	10
I feel depressed and worthless	1	2	3	4	5	6	7	8	9	10

Now that you have completed this checklist, what do you see?

_____

_____

_____

Are there specific patterns in your behaviors?

_____

_____

_____

For any questions you answered 6 or higher, what specific behaviors can you engage in to help prevent relapse?

Examples:

Warning Sign	Preventative Behavior
No interest in my appearance	When I dress in the morning, dress with the attitude that clean clothes represent clean recovery. Throw away pants with holes. Wash clothes twice weekly.

Recognize relapse warnings
Identify self-care strategies

Today, I am grateful for _____

Came . . . Came to . . . Came to Believe

More addicts have experienced recovery in Twelve Step programs than in any other single source. All of the Twelve Step programs have a spiritual basis. The willingness to accept a Higher Power is often the major stumbling block for addicts in recovery. Step Two says, *"Came to believe that a Power greater than ourselves could restore us to sanity."*

"Came to believe" suggests that your spiritual discovery is a journey. You do not need to feel as though you should have already arrived or that you need to arrive by a certain time or date. Your sense of journey may have already begun. It may be about to start. The important point is that you have a willing spirit.

Spiritual Vision

Complete the following exercise.

Do you believe there is a power greater than yourself?

☐ Yes   ☐ No

Explain:

_____

_____

_____

_____

_____

_____

To heal from pain and conflict in our life, we need to have faith in something outside of ourselves. For many people, the faith may be in a Higher Power or God. Others aren't sure. While you may be agnostic or have little faith in anything outside yourself, be open to "not always controlling" and try to develop faith. Trust that in time, healing and self-love will become a part of your life.

If you are experiencing conflict with this aspect of recovery, answers to the following questions may offer some important insights.

Did you attend a church or synagogue as a child? If so, name and describe. If not, what was the message in your family about this being unimportant as a value?

_____

_____

_____

If you were involved in a particular faith as a child, describe your involvement. Was it:

Fun?	☐ Yes	☐ No
Scary?	☐ Yes	☐ No
Boring?	☐ Yes	☐ No
Meaningful?	☐ Yes	☐ No

What was your concept of God?

Loving?	☐ Yes	☐ No
Punishing?	☐ Yes	☐ No
Indifferent?	☐ Yes	☐ No
Other?	☐ Yes	☐ No

Did you have a choice about whether or not you attended a church or synagogue?

☐ Yes ☐ No

If your involvement in your faith has stopped, how was that decision made?

_____

_____

_____

As a child or teenager, were there any particular rituals or ceremonies that were of special value or significance for you?

☐ Yes   ☐ No

What were they?

_____

_____

_____

How were they special?

_____

_____

_____

What does your Higher Power look like at this time? (You are welcome to draw or paint a portrait of your image.)

_____

_____

_____

_____

_____

_____

_____

_____

_____

_____

Now that you have completed these questions, what thoughts or reflections do you have?

_____

_____

_____

_____

_____

_____

_____

_____

_____

**Recognize impact of spiritual history
Create vision of a Higher Power**

Today, I am grateful for _____

Packing for the Spiritual Journey

Footprints

One night a man had a dream. He dreamed he was walking along the beach with the Lord. Across the sky flashed scenes from his life. For each scene, he noticed two sets of prints on the sand; one belonged to him and the other to the Lord.

When the last scene of his life flashed before him, he looked back at the footprints in the sand. He noticed that many times along the path of his life there was only one set of footprints. He also noticed that it happened at the very lowest and saddest times in his life.

This really bothered him and he questioned the Lord about it. "Lord…you said that once I decided to follow you, you'd walk with me all the way. But I have noticed that during the most troublesome times in my life there is only one set of footprints. I don't understand why you'd leave me when I needed you most."

The Lord replied, "My precious, precious child, I love you and I would never leave you. During your times of trial and suffering, when you see only one set of footprints, it was then I carried you."

—Author Unknown

Identify three times in your life you believe you were carried.

1) _____

2) _____

3) _____

Spiritual growth is a journey that continues throughout our lifetime. When our spiritual life is out of balance, everything is out of balance. A belief in a Higher Power rarely comes instantly. It does not strike like a lightning bolt. Faith is achieved through one's daily activities. Just like our physical bodies require regular exercise and proper diet to maintain our health, our spirituality needs regular nourishment and exercise to remain healthy.

Step Two from the Twelve Steps of Alcoholics Anonymous says:
"Came to believe that a Power greater than ourselves could restore us to sanity."

This Step can be broken down into the following pieces:

Came	➡	means	➡	*Show Up*
Came to	➡	means	➡	*Open Mind*
Came to believe	➡	means	➡	*Trust in a Higher Power*

Step Two is achieved by taking small, calming steps on an enlightening journey. The journey does not lead to a destination or end point called spiritual life. Rather, there are many spiritual rewards along the pathway. The payoff comes in making the journey, not reaching a destination.

Spiritual Journey

The exercise below is designed to increase your awareness about your own spiritual pathway.

Check any items that describe your spiritual pathway.

- ☐ Music / singing
- ☐ Quiet, solitude
- ☐ Appreciating nature
- ☐ Loving others unselfishly
- ☐ Listening to others
- ☐ Sharing your feelings
- ☐ Keeping a journal
- ☐ Forgiving others
- ☐ Attending a church, synagogue or other place of worship
- ☐ Praising others
- ☐ Smiling, laughing
- ☐ Reading, learning
- ☐ Helping others

☐ Sharing experiences
☐ Asking for forgiveness
☐ Embracing loved ones
☐ Twelve Steps
☐ Meditation
☐ Other Spiritual practice

Why are these pathways important for you?

_____

_____

_____

_____

_____

_____

_____

_____

_____

_____

_____

_____

What things in your life block you from your spiritual path?

_____

_____

_____

Write a want ad for the Higher Power that you would like to have in your life. Ideally, a Higher Power should be someone or something you can trust and that can help you.

_____

_____

_____

_____

_____

Name five other qualities or characteristics you would look for in a Higher Power.

1) _____

2) _____

3) _____

4) _____

5) _____

**Achieve greater serenity
Increase clarity of spiritual path**

Today, I am grateful for _____

110

Behind Closed Doors

Relapse can be the consequence of hanging on to secrets. Common secrets of the addict may be about sexual orientation, past sexual activities, criminal activities, other addictive behaviors, financial difficulties, and/or other areas of life that may feel too painful to reveal to others.

- James, in conflict about telling his home group he was gay, eventually relapsed in his eating disorder.

- Susan, after nine months of recovery from her cocaine addiction, relapsed when her boyfriend threatened to tell her husband of their affair.

- Gary had seven years of sobriety from cocaine. He actively participated in a recovery program. But in those years he continued to secretly gamble, creating more and more debt that he was hiding from his family. Unable to cope with the stress of his gambling debts and his resultant lying, he resumed his use of drugs.

- Tina has been sober for three years; her daughter turned eight and Tina relapsed. When Tina was eight, her father molested her. This is a memory she had repressed and is now fighting to keep down.

- Sam is in recovery from his sex addiction. He never disclosed a previous prostitution charge while he was active in his disease. The fear his wife will discover his secret led to his relapse.

Secrets are defined as information that is:

> Kept hidden from knowledge or view; concealed
>
> Dependably discreet
>
> Operating in a hidden or confidential manner
>
> Not expressed

We learned as children what secrets were and how to keep them. As we played and interacted with friends and family, we often learned that secrets were fun to keep. When we learned information that others may not have known, we felt special and important. But most addicts are raised in troubled families where hurtful secrets abound.

Secrets

As children we may have been solicited to keep secrets that made us feel as if we were doing something wrong or shameful. Perhaps we saw our mother or father pouring alcohol into their morning coffee or orange juice. Our parent might have said, "Be mommy or daddy's big boy or girl and don't tell anyone about this." This put us in a situation where we were asked to keep a secret that we may or may not have known was wrong to keep. In this situation, we felt a great deal of internal conflict because we were worried about the possible harmful consequences of not telling someone else. Regardless, we didn't want our parent to be angry with us, so we kept the secret.

The circumstances of our situation may have been different. Maybe we kept the secret from our friends that our family member(s) had an addiction. Maybe the secret was about mom or dad having an affair. Whatever the case, the end results were the same. We felt afraid that our parents or someone else significant in our lives would be angry with us. If this happened, we probably feared that we would be punished, hit, or yelled at for not keeping their secret(s). We learned to keep secrets so well as children, that today we often still carry some of those secrets.

As children, we may have learned how secrets work in an overt and/or covert manner. We may have been explicitly told not to talk to anyone else about how our family dynamics functioned.

"My mother used to come and cry in my bedroom at night after my father had hit her," Mary confessed. When I would ask why she wouldn't leave him or report him to the police, my mother would quickly compose herself. She would tell me, 'your father just has a small problem with his anger. I don't want anything bad to happen to him.'" In Mary's family, she learned overtly that she had to be the keeper of the family secret and the family shame.

In Ron's family keeping the secret was more covert. "Sometimes after school, my friends would come over to play. By this time of the day, my dad had been drinking for several hours. Often, he would be passed out on the couch when my friends and I came home after school. When my friends would ask what was wrong with my dad, I would say he had a migraine headache and had to take medication. No one ever had to tell me that I needed to make excuses for my dad. I instinctively knew that was what I had to do." Ron became the keeper of the family secret and the family shame.

There is a great distinction between a confidence and a secret. As children, we may have been asked to keep the details of a surprise birthday party or vacation from others. We were being asked to keep a *confidence*. If others found out, there may be disappointment or loss of the surprise element. We kept the confidence because we wanted to, not because we knew we had to.

As children, we often instinctively knew that keeping secrets was not even a choice. It was a matter of personal or family survival. We were being asked to contain the emotional energy and shame embodied in the secret. There could be overwhelming negative consequences if others found out the secret.

Secrets are handed down from one generation to another. Secrets are pieces of information that are withheld from others, often out of shame, and many times with the intent to protect someone—yourself or another. Secrets are powerful because they can control you. Very often, the primary problem of a secret is not the content of the secret itself, but what you must do to keep the secret information out of sight.

Two examples of secrets in my family of origin are:

1) _____

2) _____

It was important for me to keep these secrets because:

1) _____

2) _____

What I had to do to keep these secrets was *(specific actions)*:

_____

_____

_____

Secrets carry a great deal of power and control. An individual in a family system is confronted with the content of the secret and having to keep the secret from family members, friends, or society. Carrying a secret is a tremendous burden. There is a great deal of shame inherent in having to keep secrets. As the keeper of the secret(s), we feel shame regarding the family member we are keeping the secret about and ourselves. We may feel that our value as a person is in question by being a member of such a family.

Many of us have held on to secrets from our history for an extended period of time to avoid shame and possible social or legal consequences. By keeping these secrets, we are reinforcing our inner core of shame. Shame is the inner belief that we have little or no value as a person. Having a shame core means that we feel at the very core of our existence that we are worthless.

When our shame core is triggered, our emotional and spiritual pain can become so great that we need to re-engage in our addictive behaviors as a form of self-medication. Letting go of our secrets is crucial to staying in sobriety and preventing relapse.

What secrets are you carrying today? If the word *secrets* seems too strong, what is it no one else knows about you?

1) _____
2) _____
3) _____
4) _____
5) _____
6) _____
7) _____
8) _____

Specific personal secrets I would like to release are:

1) _____
2) _____
3) _____
4) _____
5) _____
6) _____
7) _____
8) _____

Completing this exercise took a tremendous amount of courage to move from a place of secrecy to a place of wanting to be free of secrets. Remember that the sharing of secrets is not an all-or-nothing phenomena ("I've never told anyone, now I need to tell everyone"). It is important to be able to decide who is and who is not appropriate to release secrets to.

These questions may be helpful in determining the appropriateness of revealing particular secrets.

> What would you like to share?
>
> With whom do you want to share this secret?
>
> Why do you want to share this information with this person?
>
> What do you hope will be the result?
>
> How realistic is that expectation?
>
> If the expectation is unrealistic, what is a more realistic expectation?

When wanting to release secrets, it is often very helpful to ask our sponsor and/or therapist to help us go through the above questions. When we have answered them, we can then begin a plan of the appropriate circumstances under which to reveal the secret(s).

Here are some potential guidelines for releasing secrets:

- Releasing the secret is for your benefit and not to get even with someone.
- Think through the potential results of releasing the secret(s).
- Think of how detailed you want your disclosure to be.
- Make sure the details of the secret to be revealed are correct to the best of your knowledge.
- Write out a plan for sharing the secret. What is the setting, the time of day? Who is present? Go back and review previous guidelines.

Disclosure about one's addictive behavior is vital in recovery. Yet it is not suggested that one discloses without the assistance of a professional addictions counselor to determine what is and is not appropriate. Disclosure is most healthy when the person on the receiving end is also involved in a treatment or recovery process.

Who do you need to share more openly with? Write down their names.

_____

_____

What feelings come up as you think about the secrets you've been carrying? (Examples of feelings include pain, fear, loneliness, anger, guilt, and shame.)

What thoughts and feelings came up for you while completing this exercise?

Please remember that as we get honest about our secrets, many feelings may come up for us:

> Pain about past abuses we have suffered, about our behaviors
> Fear about what will happen if we tell others about the secret(s)
> Anger about being abused, being abusive
> Guilt about our mistakes
> Shame that if others know our secrets they will really know we are worthless

Several tools can be used to support us when we are feeling overwhelmed with these and other feelings:

- Go to a meeting—this is an excellent place to feel supported without conditions

- Talk to your sponsor—he or she can offer perspective and support

- Talk to your therapist—they also help to explore issues and be supportive

- Pray—talking to your Higher Power reminds you that you are not alone—now or ever

- Meditate—connecting with self helps one to feel grounded and calm

- Say positive affirmations—these help to focus on positive statements rather than negative ones

Now that we are becoming more aware of our secrets and what it has cost us to keep them, we may have the urge to "tell all" to family members, children, spouses, and others. We may want to be sure that we don't spend even one more day hanging on to these secrets.

Revealing all of our secrets can be a damaging process to others and ourselves. Certain secrets may be appropriate for revealing immediately, while others may not be appropriate to reveal to certain people at this time, if ever.

Distinguish difference between a confidence and a secret

Recognize role of secrets

Identify secrets important to share

Identify healthy guidelines to revealing secrets

Today, I am grateful for _____

Suit Up and Show Up

We, as addicts, are accustomed to a life filled with chaos and unpredictability. In fact, this is often the way life has always been. We may have come from a home environment filled with turmoil, addictions, abuse, and a variety of other dynamics. Whether or not that was a part of our early life experiences, the rule today may be that there are no rules. Each day has no plan and is filled with insanity, high excitement, and little or no time to get things done. We may like living on the edge and feeling little or no responsibility in our lives. We become addicted to the chaos, to the rush.

A life in recovery means that we live a *balanced* life; a life with some structure and moderation. We no longer live moment to moment in the insanity that surrounds addictions. Instead, we strive to live a serene and calm life, which nurtures us in our ongoing recovery. To do this, we need to learn how to schedule and plan our lives.

This doesn't mean that every waking moment needs to be controlled and accounted for. What it means is having a flexible plan for what our day may look like and how that day will be based in recovery. We only need to plan *One Day at a Time*.

Knowing your schedule helps to identify how much time is spent working, in relationships, in leisure, and where recovery fits in with the rest of your life.

Take a look at your schedule. Describe your day in detail.

Today, when I first woke up, I

_____

_____

_____

To get ready for my day, I

_____

_____

_____

Daily Schedule

Continue to describe what your day looked like during these time periods—where you were, who you were with, what you were doing.

9 A.M. _____

_____

_____

Noon _____

_____

_____

3 P.M. _____

_____

_____

5 P.M. _____

_____

_____

7 P.M. _____

_____

_____

9 P.M. _____

_____

_____

Bedtime _____

_____

_____

Repeat this exercise for the two previous days.

How much time was devoted to recovery practice (Twelve Step meetings, reading recovery literature, meditation, talking to others in recovery)?

_____

_____

_____

Were you able to get your recovery needs met?

_____

_____

_____

Did your behavior demonstrate that sobriety was your number one priority? Explain.

_____

_____

_____

_____

_____

Were there any significant aspects of your life that you were not able to give time to?

_____

_____

_____

Identify any large periods of unaccounted time. Our addictions often consumed most of our time. Now that we are in recovery, we may have large gaps in our day. Having a schedule helps us to see that we need to fill in these spaces with positive activities that support our recovery. Use this daily log as a way to monitor how you balance your day for the next week.

Finally, ask yourself these questions:

On a daily basis, what do I need to do to keep myself sober?

_____

_____

_____

_____

_____

_____

What do I need to do today, specifically, to keep myself sober?

_____

_____

_____

_____

_____

_____

Make recovery my first priority

**Be accountable to
the practice of recovery**

Today, I am grateful for _____

First Things First

Using the circle below, divide it into pieces representing your specific priorities in life. For example, if your job and family were of equal importance in your life, and there were no other priorities, then each would have an equal half of the circle.

Now that you have prioritized this circle, what piece or pieces are the biggest?

_____

What piece or pieces are the smallest?

_____

How big a piece is your program of recovery?

_____

How do the pieces of your circle need to change to support you in recovery?

_____

_____

_____

If this circle were to represent how you prioritize your recovery, how would it be divided up?

How much of the time would be spent at meetings?

_____

How much of the time would be spent reading recovery materials?

_____

How much of the time would be spent meditating and connecting with your Higher Power?

_____

How much time would be spent socializing with others in Twelve Step recovery?

_____

The purpose of this exercise is to help identify where recovery fits in our life. For many addicts, recovery is not the number one priority. We often find ourselves focusing on other aspects of life that were neglected due to our addiction and prioritize them over recovery practice. We become complacent about what it takes to maintain recovery. In order to stay sober and prevent a relapse, *One Day at a Time* recovery needs to be the most important priority in your life. If your job, school, family, or anything else comes before your sobriety, then your program of recovery is in serious jeopardy and that sabotages your job, school, family, etc. If you were to relapse, what quality of life would you have to dedicate to your job, family, or school?

What would a realistic list of priorities look like now?

1) _____

2) _____

3) _____

4) _____

5) _____

6) _____

7) _____

8) _____

What will help you to keep recovery your number one priority?

_____

_____

_____

_____

_____

Recognize priorities
Prioritize recovery practice

Today, I am grateful for _____

Peace of Mind

One of the most healing elements of any Twelve Step program is connection with our Higher Power. This connects to our selves, to others, to our spirituality and to a power greater than us. Prayer and meditation are two excellent tools to help with this connection.

Remember that your relationship with your Higher Power is your own. Through prayer and meditation, we are able to establish a rich relationship, which helps nourish ongoing recovery.

There are a number of excellent books on meditation available. These include:

- <u>Step by Step</u>, Muriel Zink, Ballantine Books
- <u>Yesterday's Tomorrow</u>, Barry L., Hazelden Publications
- <u>Touchstones</u>, Hazelden Publications
- <u>The Promise of a New Day</u>, Karen Casey, Martha Vanceburg, Hazelden Publications
- <u>Answers in the Heart</u>, Hazelden Publications
- <u>Day by Day</u>, Hazelden Publications
- <u>Each Day a New Beginning</u>, Hazelden Publications

While many meditation audiotapes and CD's are available in bookstores, you will also appreciate Claudia Black's *Imageries* and *Letting Go Imageries*.

You may want to purchase a book, audiotape or CD to help you begin this process. It is also valuable to be able to develop your own meditations. This comes with practice.

Below is an example of a spirituality meditation and visualization. Remember that this is only *a* way to meditate, not *the* way. This meditation process may feel awkward at first if you haven't experienced mediation before, but it can be highly valuable if you allow yourself to relax and be open to the process. Read it through a few times, then try it. You might also record it to your own selection of music.

Find a comfortable sitting position, uncross your arms and legs, and begin to take slow deep breaths in and out. Gently sit back and close your eyes.

Begin to breathe slowly and deeply.

Focus on your breathing.

Take a deep breath in… and out.

Take a deep breath in… and out.

As you breathe in, visualize your Higher Power filling you with healing and protective light.

As you breathe out, visualize stress, tension, worry and fear leaving your body. Continue to breathe in and out.

Slowly become aware of your head and neck.

Feel your tension melting away and feel your head and neck begin to relax.

Feel this relaxation slowly moving down through your shoulders as you continue to breathe in healing light and energy.

Feel the relaxation move down into your arms and chest.

Know that you are safe and you are loved.

Breathe in… and out.

Breathe in… and out.

Feel the relaxation moving down into your waist and legs.

Feel the tension and stress leaving your body.

Feel the relaxation moving down into your feet.

Feel your connection to the earth and the connection to your Higher Power.

As you continue to breathe deeply, imagine a place where you feel completely safe and serene. This may be the mountains, the beach, the forest.

Wherever this place is, it is your place to be. Imagine yourself there right now.

Take a look around and focus on what you see.

What do you smell?

What do you hear?

Let all of your senses experience the serenity and safety of this special place.

Know that this is your place that you can come to at any time.

Slowly begin to visualize how your Higher Power might look and feel.

Let the image begin to fill your mind, body, and spirit.

Imagine your body and spirit being filled with serenity, contentment and peace.

Feel your spirit connecting with your Higher Power.

Feel the infinite wisdom and love your Higher Power has for you.

Feel the safety and protection it offers you.

Know that your Higher Power guides your path in recovery and is with you at all times.

Know that you can connect with your Higher Power and your safe place any time you choose through prayer and meditation.

Know that you are not alone in your recovery.

You are surrounded by love and support if you choose to let it in.

As you continue to breathe, gently become aware of your body.

Become aware of your head… your neck… your shoulders and arms.

Become aware of your back… your chest… your waist… your legs… your feet.

Become aware of your connection to the earth.

When you are ready, open your eyes.

Use tools to facilitate meditation and prayer

Today, I am grateful for _____

Good vs. Best

Many addicts ask, *"What is the difference between abstinence and sobriety?"*

Abstinence means that we have stopped engaging in our addictive behaviors. It has been said that if you sober up a drunk safe cracker, what you have is a sober safe cracker. Abstinence is not just refraining from our addictive behaviors; it's a return to a healthy lifestyle.

If we decided to only stop our using behaviors without getting into a program of recovery, we would have stopped our addictive behaviors, but changed nothing else. This is where the expression "Dry Drunk" comes from. The alcoholic stops drinking, but continues on in their insane and chaotic behavior because they are not using any new living tools.

When we make a conscious choice to stop our addictive behaviors, we have on some level decided that we want a life free from the pain and chaos we have known while we were out drinking, drugging, eating, sexing, gambling, *fill in your addiction.* Sobriety is refraining from our addictive behavior, but it is also refraining from distorted and addictive thinking. It is learning skills that allow us a healthy lifestyle.

We come to experience that life isn't always characterized by pain and chaos. This doesn't mean that life won't have its trying moments. There is a recovery saying to remind us of how serenity can be present for us even under fire:

"Recovery doesn't always mean safety from the storm. It means safety during the storm."

In what areas of my life am I abstinent?

_____

_____

_____

In what areas of my life am I sober?

_____

_____

_____

In what ways can I improve my sobriety?

_____

_____

_____

In what ways can I improve my serenity?

_____

_____

_____

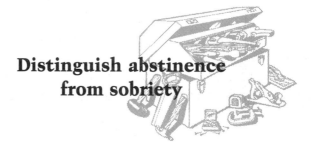

**Distinguish abstinence
from sobriety**

Today, I am grateful for _____

But Wait . . . There's More

Now that you have completed this guide, what are the signals or warnings you need to watch for in light of what you are learning about yourself? Remember that knowledge of how your own addictive process works is a powerful tool and ally for your recovery. The more information you gather about what specific factors may lead to your relapse the more resources you have to help you identify specific solutions.

The disease of addiction is based upon the thinking that we, as addicts, are invincible. It is extremely important to identify specific warning signs to a relapse and have a well-prepared relapse prevention plan. If these signs begin to appear, you do not need to think about what to do, but need to act immediately and call upon the resources previously identified.

Imagine this:

You are living in your house, apartment, etc., and you have thought ahead to what you would do in case of emergencies such as fire, flood, tornado, hurricane, or earthquake. You have a very specific plan in the event that any one of these situations should occur. Now, imagine that one of these situations is actually occurring. You would not stand and analyze how and why you are there, you would take immediate action to protect yourself and save your life. Think of relapse prevention in the same way. You need a specific plan to protect your life in recovery should you find yourself in harm's way.

Identify what you believe are the most critical relapse contributors to your recovery:

1) _____

2) _____

3) _____

4) _____

Now list what you need to do to prevent a relapse if/when these signals occur. Be specific.

1) _____

2) _____

3) _____

4) _____

5) _____

6) _____

7) _____

8) _____

Identify six names and phone numbers of people you could call should you be experiencing a relapse trigger. Be realistic. Who are you most apt to reach?

NAME	PHONE #
1)	
2)	
3)	
4)	
5)	
6)	

What will you do if you cannot contact them?

_____

_____

_____

Are you carrying a meeting book in your car, your motorcycle, bicycle? Is there one at work, school and at home?

_____

If I relapse, whom do I call? Do not just consider a relapse the resumption of your addiction. You must also consider the self-defeating behavior that is a relapse trigger.

NAME	PHONE #
1)	
2)	
3)	
4)	
5)	
6)	

Make sure that you keep this relapse emergency plan with you at all times. In order for the emergency plan to work, you need access to it.

An Emergency Plan only works if you put it into action immediately when you begin to see warning signs. They may even be small warning signs like attending fewer meetings, not calling your sponsor as often, an increase in controlling behavior, a heightened attitude of over confidence, hanging onto resentments, etc. Whatever the signs may be, these are precisely the times that you need the plan to help protect your precious sobriety.

Identify critical relapse contributors
Have specific emergency plan

Today, I am grateful for _____

ONE WAY ➤ **Same Song, Second Verse, Same Theme**

I

I walk down the street.
> There is a deep hole in the sidewalk.
> I fall in.
> I am lost ... I am helpless.
> > It isn't my fault.
It takes forever to find a way out.

Kathryn is a homemaker. In spite of raising three daughters, she became bored as a homemaker and gradually found herself creating excuses to be in social circles where people drank, used cocaine, and partied. This led to outside sexual affairs. At the age of thirty-three, with her husband threatening to leave her if she did not stop her behavior, she sought treatment and began a recovery process.

II

I walk down the same street.
> There is a deep hole in the sidewalk.
> I pretend I don't see it.
> I fall in again.
I can't believe I am in the same place
> > but it isn't my fault.
It still takes a long time to get out.

Kathryn was active in a recovery program for a couple of years. She enjoyed the fellowship, the women's meetings, and she had a sponsor. But she only shared at an intimate level with her sponsor. It was here she would talk, for the first time, about having been chronically sexually abused as a child. She gradually found herself becoming preoccupied with health issues and received a lot of attention for what seemed to be repetitive and severe health problems. Her first relapse occurred with an addiction to prescription pain pills. After one year of actively using, she was detoxed and once again sought out Twelve Step programs.

III

I walk down the same street.
    There is a deep hole in the sidewalk.
    I see it is there.
    I still fall in ... it's a habit.
      My eyes are open.
      I know where I am.
It is my fault.
I get out immediately.

For the next year and a half, Kathryn's recovery followed the same pattern as the first time. She embraced the women's fellowship, had the same sponsor with whom she would continue to talk about the sexual abuse, and once again became preoccupied about what appeared to be self-imposed health issues. She relapsed again. Three years later she detoxed and again came back to the same group and sponsor.

Mark took a similar journey.

I

I walk down the street.
    There is a deep hole in the sidewalk.
    I fall in.
    I am lost ... I am helpless.
      It isn't my fault.
It takes forever to find a way out.

Mark began his addictive behavior as a teenager. His first treatment experience was just after high school graduation when his parents insisted he go. After treatment, he attended self-help meetings and liked them. He talked in meetings and was most verbal about his need for a job. He finally got a job. His first goal was to buy a car — which he did within months. By this time he had fallen in love. In his mind, all was going great and then he relapsed. Within weeks, he lost his job, his girlfriend, and wrecked his uninsured car. His parents paid a second time to send him to treatment.

II

I walk down the same street.
    There is a deep hole in the sidewalk.
    I pretend I don't see it.
    I fall in again.
I can't believe I am in the same place
      but it isn't my fault.
It still takes a long time to get out.

Mark was glad to be back with his recovery friends. He was chagrined about what happened and determined to not let that occur again. Within a month, he clearly needed a job and he had to have a car to get around. His friends heard about his remorse, his struggles with day-to-day living, and before long he had a job and a car. He met a young woman, and again, this was the love of his life. Aware of what happened last time, he knew he couldn't be complacent about his recovery. Yet, he became very busy… and he relapsed.

III

I walk down the same street.
> There is a deep hole in the sidewalk.
> I see it is there.
> I still fall in … it's a habit.
>> My eyes are open.
>> I know where I am.
> It is my fault.
> I get out immediately.

No one saw Mark for a long time until one day he showed up very distressed, just out of treatment again. He went to a lot of meetings, talked about his remorse over what had happened and expressed his gratefulness for his parents who had once again paid for treatment. He was thankful for his friends; they helped him follow job leads and he met another woman. As much as he cared for this woman, when she became pregnant he was not sure what to do. This all began to feel familiar. Would he be able to make some changes before he started to use again?

To move from Chapter Three to Four and Five, it is important to identify any repetitive patterns to a history of relapse. It is quite possible you are repeating behavior that is not moving towards recovery or (is) sabotaging recovery. While certainly not a complete list, the following are some common repetitive issues for you to consider.

Choice of friends

Choice of sponsor

Participation in recovery meetings

How much you listen

Practice service work

Priorities

Behavior in relationships

Attitude — such as complacency, argumentativeness, impatience, etc.

What you are *not* discussing

Identify your repetitious patterns.

1) _____

2) _____

3) _____

4) _____

5) _____

6) _____

7) _____

8) _____

In asking addicts with various disorders what they needed to do differently to move from the third to the fourth and then to the fifth chapter of "A Hole in the Sidewalk," they identified:

Accept being an addict

Get a sponsor

Follow direction

Go to more meetings

Listen to others

Prioritize recovery over being in a relationship

Prioritize recovery over work

Quit going to places where they used or acted out

Limit and let go of certain relationships

Quit accepting family enabling

Dump emotional baggage

Tell the truth

Reach out for help even when not sure it is needed

Share both the good and the bad at meetings

Find ways to help others and not be so self-focused

Quit putting expectations on recovery

Identify what you see yourself doing differently that will allow you to get to Chapter Five of "A Hole in the Sidewalk."

_____

_____

_____

_____

_____

_____

_____

_____

Let's conclude this journey with another look at Kathryn and Mark.

Kathryn came back to the same group and the same sponsor. When her sponsor suggested she see a psychotherapist to address her sexual abuse, she did. She identified her chronic use of prescription pills and it's connection to her need to see doctors. She expanded her recovery program to include additional types of meetings. Willingness, change in behavior, and insight would lead to her ability to walk around the hole in the sidewalk. Ultimately she saw the need to walk down a different street.

Mark was about to be a father and became aware he needed to make some choices. He became less preoccupied with his love affair, material gains and the need to look good. He found himself wanting to talk at a deeper level with his sponsor and at meetings. He began hearing things differently than before. He sought out additional recovering friends. He took responsibility for allowing himself to be rescued by his parent's money and began to pay them back. He had begun to walk around the hole and while it would take more time, ultimately he would walk down a different street.

IV

<blockquote>
I walk down the same street.
There is a deep hole in the sidewalk.
I walk around it.
</blockquote>

V

<blockquote>
I walk down another street.
</blockquote>

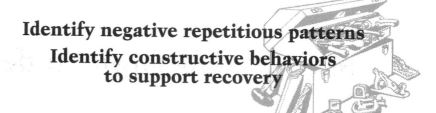

Identify negative repetitious patterns
Identify constructive behaviors
to support recovery

Today, I am grateful for _____

May you walk down a different street.

Resources

There are currently several million recovering people around the planet attending Twelve Step meetings on a regular basis. It is relatively easy to find a meeting in any city or country if you know where to look. The World Wide Web provides a variety of recovery resources; these may change, so please check your search engines if the links do not work.

The following is a directory of Twelve Step organizations.

Alcoholics Anonymous
Box 459 Grand Central Station
NYC, NY 10163
212.870.3400
www.alcoholics-anonymous.org

Alanon / Alateen
1600 Corporate Landing Pkwy
Virginia Beach, VA 23454
800.344.2666 (option #3) meeting info only
757.563.1600 / 888.4ALANON
www.al-anon.org
www.al-anon.org/alateen.html

Adult Children of Alcoholics
PO Box 3216
Torrance, CA 90510
310.534.1815
www.adultchildren.org

Co-dependents Anonymous
PO Box 670861 (meetings info)
Dallas, TX 75367-0861
706.648.6868 World Service Office
www.codependents.org

COSA (Co-Sex Addicts Anonymous)
National Services
612.537.6904
www2.shore.net/~cosa

Debtors Anonymous
PO Box 888 (World Services Office)
Needham, MA 02492-0009
781.453.2743
212.969.8111 (greater NY area)
www.debtorsanonymous.org

Eating Addictions Anonymous
www.dcregistry.com/users/eatingaddictions

Emotions Anonymous
www.emotionsanonymous.org

Families Anonymous
PO Box 3475
Culver City, CA 90231-3475
818.989.7841
800.736.9805
www.familiesanonymous.org

Gamblers Anonymous
PO Box 17173
Los Angeles, CA 90017
213.386.8789
www.gamblersanonymous.org

Marijuana Anonymous
www.marijuana-anonymous.org

Narcotics Anonymous
www.na.orgj

Cocaine Anonymous
PO Box 2000 (World Services Office)
Suite 100
310.559.5833
www.ca.org

Nat. Council on Alcoholism & Drug Dependence
12 W 21ˢᵗ St
NYC, NY 10010
212.206.6770
www.ncadd.org

Nicotine Anonymous
www.nicotine-anonymous.org

Overeaters Anonymous
6075 Zenith Court
Rio Rancho. NM 87174
505.8912664
www.overeatersanonymous.org

Pills Anonymous
PO Box 772
Bronx, NY 10451
212.874.0700
http://club.yahoo.com/clubs/pillsanonymous

Rational Recovery System
Box 800
Lotus, CA 95651
530.621.4374
800.303.2873
www.rational.org/recovery

Recovering Couples Anonymous
PO Box 11872
St Louis, MO 63105
314.397.0867
www.recovering-couples.org
Baltimore, MD 21222-6817
S-Anon
PO Box 111242
Nashville, TN 37222-1242
615.833.3152
www.sanon.org

National Assoc. for Children of Alcoholics
Los Angeles, CA 90049-800011426 Rockville Pike
Rockville, MD 20852
301.468.0985
888.554.2627
www.health.org/nacoa

Sex Addicts Anonymous
PO Box 70949
Houston, TX 77270
800.477.8191
www.sexaa.org

Sexaholics Anonymous (SA)
International Central Office
PO Box 300
Simi Valley, CA 93602
www.sa.org

Sexual Compulsives Anonymous (SCA)
West Coast
PO Box 4470
170 Sunset Blvd #520
Los Angeles, CA 90027
310.859.5585
East Coast
PO Box 1585
Old Chelsea Station
NYC, NY 10011
212.429.1123
www.sca-recovery.org

Sex & Love Addicts Anonymous (SLAA)
PO Box 338
Norwood, MA 02062-0338
781.255.8825
www.slaafws.org

Survivors of Incest Anonymous
PO Box 21817 (World Service Office)

410.282.3400
www.siawso.org

Women for Sobriety & Men for Sobriety
PO Box 618
Quakertown, PA 18951
215.536.8026
www.womenforsobirety.org

Also by Claudia Black, Ph.D.

Changing Course
It Will Never Happen to Me
The Missing Piece
Repeat After Me
My Dad Loves Me My Dad Has A Disease
It's Never Too Late To Have A Happy Childhood
Imageries CD
Letting Go Imageries CD

We welcome you to our Online Catalog
www.claudiablack.com

Claudia Black's
Books — Audios — Videos
available through

MAC Publishing
PMB 346
321 High School Road N.E.
Bainbridge Island, WA 98110
206.842.6303 Voice • 206.842.6235 Fax